The Radical Lives of Helen Keller

The History of Disability

A series edited by Paul K. Longmore and Lauri Umansky

The New Disability History: American Perspectives
Paul K. Longmore and Lauri Umansky

Reflections: The Life and Writings of a Young Blind Woman
in Post-Revolutionary France
Edited and translated by Catherine J. Kudlick and Zina Weygand

Signs of Resistance: American Deaf Cultural History, 1900 to World War II
Susan Burch

The Radical Lives of Helen Keller
Kim E. Nielsen

The Radical Lives
of Helen Keller

Kim E. Nielsen

Consulting Editor: Harvey J. Kaye

NEW YORK UNIVERSITY PRESS

New York and London

NEW YORK UNIVERSITY PRESS
New York and London
www.nyupress.org

© 2004 by New York University
All rights reserved

Library of Congress Cataloging-in-Publication Data
Nielsen, Kim E.
The radical lives of Helen Keller / Kim E. Nielsen
p. cm. — (The history of disability series)
Includes bibliographical references and index.
ISBN 0-8147-5813-4 (hc : acid-free)
1. Helen Keller, 1880–1968.
2. Helen Keller, 1880–1968—Political and social views.
3. Blind-deaf women—United States—Biography.
4. Blind-deaf women—Education—United States.
I. Title. II. Series.
HV1624.K4N54 2003
362.4'1'092—dc21 2003014386

New York University Press books are printed on acid-free paper,
and their binding materials are chosen for strength and durability.

Manufactured in the United States of America

10 9 8 7 6 5 4 3 2 1

To Nathan

Contents

Acknowledgments

Unlike previous Hellen Keller biographers, I come to Keller as a historian trained in women's political lives in the twentieth-century United States. As a child I did not read Keller's mythical story or connect intensely with her image. Neither am I particularly interested in Anne Sullivan Macy's education of her. Amazement with her disability and her accomplishments didn't prompt this book nor did a desire to commemorate her. My intellectual interests center around how U.S. women have justified, explained, embraced, fought for, and lived out their citizenship on personal, familial, local, and national levels. Helen Keller interests me because she was one of the most influential and widely recognized women of the twentieth century, whose primary interests were political but whose political life has been largely ignored.

The best part about writing on Helen Keller is the people I have met along the way. The generosity, intellectual energy, good spirits, and collegiality of the disability studies community are unparalleled. Paul Longmore and Lauri Umansky served as model editors, responding with good cheer to questions large and small. Susan Burch, Derek Jeffreys, Murdoch Johnson, Harvey Kaye, Linda Kerber, Brynne Thomas, and Dianne Tuff read the manuscript at pivotal moments and offered sound advice. Linn Heider is doubly talented, providing loving childcare and spotting me on the bench press. Commentators, fellow panelists, and audience members at meetings of the Organization of American Historians, Society for Disability Studies, Berkshire Conference on Women's History, Southern Historical Association, and the University of Wisconsin-System Women's Studies Conference offered insightful comments and vigorous questions. All helped to make this book better.

Without librarians, archivists, and financial assistance I could not have finished this book. Staff members at the American Foundation for the Blind gave repeated assistance cheerfully. Thanks also go to Perkins School for the Blind, the Franklin and Eleanor Roosevelt Library, and the Library of Congress. The interlibrary loan staff at the University of Wisconsin-Green Bay found every item I sought. The Franklin and Eleanor Roosevelt Institute and the University of Wisconsin-Green Bay also provided financial assistance.

Finally, as always, my deepest appreciation goes to Nathan, Morgan and Maya. They make life infinitely richer and endlessly interesting.

Timeline

1866 April 14 Anne Sullivan born

1876 February 22 Sullivan sent to Tewksbury

1880 June 27 Helen Keller born, Tuscumbia, Alabama

1880 October 7 Sullivan goes to Perkins

1882 February Keller ill

1887 March 3 Sullivan arrives in Alabama

1888 May Keller and Sullivan arrive in Boston

1889 Laura Bridgman dies

1890 Spring Keller starts oral speech lessons

1894 October Keller attends Wright-Humason School
for the Deaf

1896 August 19 Keller's father dies

1896 Keller becomes a convert to Swedenborgianism

1896 October Keller enrolls in Cambridge School
for Young Ladies to prepare for Radcliffe

1900 Keller enters Radcliffe

1903 *The Story of My Life*

1904 June Keller graduates from Radcliffe cum laude

1904 moves to Wrentham, Massachusetts

1905 May 2 John and Anne marry

1906 Keller appointed to Massachusetts Commission
for the Blind

1908 *The World I Live In*

1909 Keller joins Socialist Party

1910 *The Song of the Stone Wall*

1912 Lawrence, Massachusetts textile strike

1913 May John Macy leaves for Europe

1914 *Out of the Dark*

1914 Anne and John Macy's relationship over

1914 Fall Polly Thomson joins Keller/Sullivan team

1916 February NAACP letter and check

1916 November Peter Fagan

1916 Sells Wrentham house

1916 Buys Forest Hills, Long Island house

1919 *Deliverance*

1920 to spring 1924 Vaudeville stage performances

1921 American Foundation for the Blind founded

1921 Keller's mother dies

1924 Robert La Follette campaign

1924 Keller and Macy join AFB

1927 Nella Braddy Henney joins team

1927 *My Religion*

1929 *Midstream*

1929 Macy's eye removed

1930 England and Scotland

1932 England and Scotland

1932 Death of John Macy

1933 England and Scotland

1933 Henney, *Anne Sullivan Macy*

1936 October 20 Anne Sullivan Macy dies

1936 November 4 Keller and Thomson leave for Scotland

1937 February 9 return to United States

1937 April 1 Leave for Japan visit—two months

1938 *Journal*

1938 Fall Sells Forest Hills house and moves to
Arcan Ridge, Westport, Connecticut

1941 Proposed trip to South America canceled by war

1943 Visits military hospitals

1944 September Keller speaks at rally with Henry Wallace
for Roosevelt in Madison Square Garden

1946 October leaves for England, Greece,
France, Italy, Ireland, The Vatican

1946 November 23 Arcan Ridge house burns

1947 Egypt, England, Syria, Lebanon, Jordan

1948 Australia, New Zealand, Japan

1950 Spring Personal trip to Davidsons in France and Italy

1950 September Herbert Haas dies

1951 South Africa

1952 Jo Davidson dies

1952 Egypt, Syria, Lebanon, Jordan, Israel, France

1953 Brazil, Chile, Peru, Panama, Mexico

1953 *The Unconquered*

1954 Ivy Green, in Tuscumbia, listed on
National Register of Historic places

1955 India, Hong Kong, Philippines, Japan

1956 *Teacher*

1956 Scotland, Portugal, Spain, France, Switzerland

1957 Canada, Iceland, Switzerland, Finland, Sweden, Norway, Denmark

1959 September Polly Thomson's stroke

1959 Stage production of *The Miracle Worker*

1960 January Break-up with Nella Braddy Henney

1960 March 21 Polly Thompson dies

1961 October Keller's first stroke

1964 Keller awarded Medal of Freedom

1968 June 1 Keller dies

Introduction

Helen Keller is a historical figure known around the globe, whose publicly celebrated story tends to begin and often ends with the moment in 1887, when Anne Sullivan pumped water onto the seven-year-old girl's hands and the manual alphabet became her main means of communication. The Helen Keller of political passion and action, the adult who did not die until 1968, is absent from *The Miracle Worker* and the warehouse quantity of children's and adult literature about her. Our shared cultural memories of her generally omit her vivid political life and politicized activities, particularly her interest in radicalism and her critique of capitalism. The sentimentalized story of the young deaf-blind girl has trumped the Helen Keller represented in Philip Foner's 1967 anthology of her socialist and radical speeches.[1] She frequently did not like the world as it was and sought political frameworks for change. The manufactured frameworks of our historical memory, no less political, keep that Helen Keller hidden from view.

Keller's first step toward our shared cultural memories came when Alexander Graham Bell first heard of the six-and-a-half-year-old child in 1886. An illness at the age of nineteen months had left her deaf and blind. From their hometown of Tuscumbia, Alabama, her parents sought assistance for the young girl they loved, since they felt increasingly incapable of parenting her. Responding to a letter from Helen's mother Kate, Bell, already famous as an inventor of the telephone and as an educator of deaf people, met with Helen, her mother, and her father Captain Arthur H. Keller. He forwarded them to Boston's Perkins School for the Blind and its director Michael Anagnos. But Bell remained, in Keller's characterization, "a wise, affectionate, and understanding friend" until the end of his life. She vacationed with the Bell family and considered him a father figure. He

1

always, she said, "considered me a capable human being, and not some sort of pitiable human ghost groping its way through the world."[2]

Bell is a controversial figure in the history of culturally Deaf people. He believed signing a primitive and subhuman form of language. In concert with others, he led the campaign to suppress the use of sign language among deaf people. He thus insisted that teaching lip reading and oralism (oral speech) to deaf people was the "greatest of all objects."[3] Keller agreed, characterizing oralism as "one of the divinest miracles of the nineteenth century."[4] In marriage, in education, and in social life, Bell therefore encouraged separating deaf people from one another in order to make sign language and Deaf culture nearly impossible. Many Deaf people, reveling in the rich Deaf culture made possible by American Sign Language (ASL) and the communities developed around Deaf institutions, resisted organizationally and personally. Many were, and are, antagonistic toward Bell and Keller for their endorsement of oralism. Using ASL, several generations of deaf children had grown to accomplish literacy and public success. When forced to use primarily oral techniques of communication rather than sign, literacy and education levels fell in the late nineteenth century.[5]

ASL is a language in which individuals use facial expressions, hand, and arm motions to signify entire concepts, just as spoken or written words signify concepts. It has its own sentence structures, verb forms, and conjunctions. Educated in an oral system, as well as an advocate for it, Keller didn't use ASL but generally finger-spelled. As she described finger-spelling, "I place my hand on the hand of the speaker so lightly as not to impede its movements. The position of the hand is as easy to feel as it is to see. I do not feel each letter any more than you see each letter separately when you read. Constant practice makes the fingers very flexible, and some of my friends spell rapidly—about as fast as an expert writes on a typewriter. The mere spelling is, of course, no more a conscious act than it is in writing."[6]

Bell considered Keller's finger-spelled English to accord with his educational views. He thought the same of her steadfast efforts to learn and use spoken English. He pushed her toward Boston's Perkins School for the

Blind because he believed educators of deaf people could do little for her and would encourage her to use sign language. He also endorsed Perkins because its staff had already successfully taught finger-spelling communication to one deaf-blind child: Laura Bridgman.

In the mid-nineteenth century, an immense theological, educational, and philosophical debate raged about the relationship between speech, intellect, and the soul. Without speech or oral input, many believed that a child would never cultivate intellect or soul—indeed, might even lack them. Teaching such a child was generally thought impossible. Boston reformer and Perkins School for the Blind director Samuel Gridley Howe searched three years for a deaf-blind child suitable to explore these issues and establish his fame. Finding seven-year-old Laura Bridgman in 1837, Howe immediately brought her to Perkins. She would remain there until her death in 1889. Bridgman, like Keller many years later, had lost her sight and hearing at a fairly young age due to illness and had appeared as a bright and creative child. Howe's success at teaching her language, and his perhaps even greater success at publicizing her, made Howe, Perkins, and Bridgman nearly world famous. Charles Dickens visited the child, chronicling her in *American Notes* (1842). Her fame reportedly surpassed that of any other woman, except the queen of England. Learning of Bridgman by reading *American Notes* prompted Keller's mother to seek an education for her daughter. For Keller's parents and for Alexander Graham Bell, the school where the by-then elderly Laura Bridgman still lived was the logical place to seek an education for the young Helen.[7] Most likely because of its encouragement of sign language, Bell ignored the possibility of the American School for the Deaf in Hartford, Connecticut, which had taught another deaf-blind child, Julia Brace.[8]

When the young Helen's parents contacted Perkins School with the help of Bell, they corresponded with Samuel Gridley Howe's son-in-law Michael Anagnos. Howe was dead, but his reputation and that of Perkins continued under Anagnos's care. Within months Anagnos arranged to send the school's star pupil, financially needy Anne Sullivan, to the couple's Tuscumbia, Alabama, home. Sullivan direly needed employment. At

Portrait of Anne Sullivan at twenty-one year of age, the year she met Keller.
Courtesy of the American Foundation for the Blind. Used with permission of the American Foundation for the Blind, Helen Keller Archives.

Portrait of Keller at the time of her Radcliffe graduation, 1904. *Courtesy of the American Foundation for the Blind. Used with permission of the American Foundation for the Blind, Helen Keller Archives.*

the age of ten, she had been orphaned by her mother and deserted by her father, both poor Irish immigrants. The courts had placed her and her brother in Massachusetts' Tewksbury Asylum, where he soon died. Anne had secured an education at Perkins only by begging touring philanthropists for assistance. Recent surgeries had improved her eyesight, but her eyes frequently caused her pain and her eyesight would fluctuate for the rest of her life. Anagnos optimistically assumed her improved vision would continue.

The Keller household had never before encountered anyone like the twenty-one-year-old Anne Sullivan nor, apparently, had the Tuscumbia community. The Kellers knew little about her. When Kate Keller and stepson James waited at the train station for her arrival in March 1887, they were joined by a crowd eager to see "the Yankee girl who was going to teach the Keller child." Sullivan purportedly hesitated to accept employment in the Keller household for fear (correctly) that the family had once owned slaves. Friends warned her not to discuss the Civil War. Once in Tuscumbia, she ignored the advice, arguing the war vigorously with Keller family members. Her criticisms ranged widely, for she went so far as to criticize the housekeeping of southern women.[9]

Not long after Sullivan taught language to the young Helen, she convinced Arthur and Kate Keller that their child would be best served at Perkins School for the Blind. The pair moved to Boston in 1888 where, until his death in 1906, Anagnos and Sullivan would continually battle over control of Helen and her public image. He needed the attractive young child, and later the charming young woman, for the publicity and funds she attracted. Like Howe with Laura Bridgman, Anagnos devoted intense efforts toward publicizing her successful education. Sullivan needed Perkins and Helen to establish her own legitimacy and maintain the funds brought by that legitimacy. If there was a doubt before, Perkins became the nation's premiere school for blind children, with Helen Keller forever linked to it.

In her massively successful 1903 autobiography, *The Story of My Life*, Keller emphasized her growing thirst for accomplishment and an education: As a child, "The thought of going to college took root in my heart and became an earnest desire." After Perkins, she and Anne Sullivan spent several years in New York, attempting to develop her lip-reading and oral speech at the Wright-Humason School for the Deaf. Her ambition was starkly apparent. Despite what she characterized as "the strong opposition of many true and wise friends," she "enter[ed] into competition for a degree with seeing and hearing girls" and sought admission to Radcliffe.[10] After several further years of preparation at the Cambridge School for Young Ladies, she entered the prestigious female counterpart of Harvard in the fall of 1900 and graduated in 1904.

Once Keller became an adult, she continued her organizational and personal linkage with blindness. As she sought a purpose, "the blind" became her primary public focus. The early efforts of Bell, the legacy of Howe and Bridgman, and the continued efforts of Anagnos and Sullivan all pushed her in that direction. Keller's early lobbying and fund-raising efforts on behalf of the American Foundation for the Blind strengthened the move. As will become apparent, few viable alternative opportunities existed.

Joining the Socialist Party of America in 1909, Keller became an advocate of female suffrage, a defender of the radical Industrial Workers of the World, and a supporter of birth control and the unemployed. She criticized World War I as a profit-making venture for industrialists and urged working-class men to resist the war. Later, she expressed alarm at the violence and weapons of World War II. She supported striking workers and jailed dissidents and expressed passionate views about the need for a just and economically equitable society. She blamed industrialization and poverty for causing disability among a disproportionately large number of working-class people. She became an inveterate fundraiser and political lobbyist. She followed international politics closely, never failing to form strong opinions on international matters. She became one of the nation's most effective but unofficial ambassadors, visiting over thirty countries. Her intimate friends knew that her most valued dinner companions, her most valued reading materials, and her favorite topics of correspondence (other than her dogs) were political in nature.

A wide array of political and social issues interested Keller deeply, though she is most intensely connected to advocacy for blind people. Why did she choose to spend most of her life energies and the public capital generated by her fame focused on advocacy for blind people? More specifically, why advocacy for the American Foundation for the Blind (AFB)? She declared in 1929 that she dedicated her life to this advocacy because she "heard the call of the sightless."[11] Alexander Graham Bell, the legacy of Laura Bridgman, Michael Anagnos of Perkins School for the Blind, and eventually the American Foundation for the Blind magnified the call. Once it was heard, Keller found it difficult to follow other life paths.

Despite Keller's intense public focus on blindness, the historical linkage of her as exclusively an advocate for blind people is not an accurate portrayal. Her interests were immense. She was deaf-blind. She loved dogs. She was female. She cared about racial and economic inequalities. She loved international politics. She opposed nuclear weapons. Throughout her entire eighty-eight years, she loved knowledge of and participation in the larger political and cultural world. Her 1956 biographer Van Wyck Brooks claimed that while she was at Perkins her interest in politics was so strong that it "puzzled" Perkins Superintendent Michael Anagnos.[12] As an adult reflecting back on her earlier years, Keller claimed to have discussed politics first with her father. Captain Keller, a regional newspaper proprietor, served in local government positions and in the Confederate army, but it is unlikely that the two discussed politics to a great extent. Her 1896 characterization of an earlier family life that included telling stories to her siblings, reading to her mother, and discussing "the political situation" with her father seems more wishful than real, particularly when one realizes that she offered the recollection in the year her father died.[13] She knew the political issues of the day while growing up largely because of the efforts of Anne Sullivan to teach the young girl about the world around her.

Until her death in 1968, political issues continued to interest Keller. She claimed and then acted upon her claimed right to hold opinions, to be present in a public space, and to think and act politically in the public sphere. Liberal democracies such as the United States operate on the premise that its citizens are educable and can make decisions about their nation by voting or with other public-sphere activities. Some of Keller's contemporaries questioned her capacity to participate in the public realm. They interpreted her disability, her gender, and sometimes her political sentiments as rendering her unfit for a wide-ranging political life. As an eager and intensely political person, she reacted with anger and frustration to the constant presumptions of her mental and physical unfitness for a public life. She frequently found such attitudes more debilitating than her disability.

As the world's most famous person with an acknowledged disability in the twentieth century, whatever Keller wrote, spoke, or did mattered. The policies and attitudes she espoused regarding people with disabilities had political, legal, medical, financial, cultural, and educational consequences. Her public persona was held up as a standard for other people with disabilities and shaped their personal and political options, whether or not she or they desired it. She understood the political implications of class. She also actively involved herself in advocating for people with disabilities. But she rarely explored the political implications of disability. For most of her life, the disability politics she adopted were frequently conservative, consistently patronizing, and occasionally repugnant. These politics regarded disability as inherently debilitating in body, mind, and spirit. They attributed the primary cause of this debilitation to physiology rather than social structures. Like Franklin Roosevelt, her life as the exception served to prove rather than contradict these political models for it framed disability as a problem to be conquered; and once conquered, a problem left behind.

Why is disability political? People with disabilities have had and continue to have lower educational rates, lower incomes, and less social influence than those considered nondisabled. People with disabilities have been and frequently continue to be denied access to public space and participation in public events. Historically, laws have denied people with disabilities marriage, education, children, employment, citizenship, and the right to be in public. People with disabilities faced and do face discrimination as a social grouping. This claim of discrimination, however, demands the difficult recognition that disability is frequently based not on physical impairment, but on the ways those with greater power in society view disability and thus construct society, both metaphorically and physically. All of us have bodies that differ, but people with physical disabilities are understood as disabled because their bodily differences are considered not only of greater consequence than the bodily differences of others but also deeply socially discrediting. Because of the economic, legal, and cultural implications, how we define disability and designate who is labeled "disabled" has powerful results. As with the case of Helen Keller, this power was highly contested.

Aided and encouraged by Anne Sullivan and the leadership of the AFB, Keller avoided contact with other people with disabilities throughout most of her life. She repeatedly turned down requests to speak to groups of Deaf people or other groups of self-organized disabled people. None of her close friends was disabled, perhaps the only exception being Japanese educator Takeo Iwahashi. Her isolation stands in sharp contrast to the politicized groups of people with disabilities that existed during her lifetime, based in friendships and social networks formed in educational institutions. It seems unlikely that Sullivan or other supporters like Alexander Graham Bell, Michael Anagnos, or AFB leader M.C. Migel would have volunteered knowledge of such networks. Nor, however, did Keller seek such information. She insisted on learning about and taking action regarding female suffrage, radical politics, oral speech, and the Christian teachings of Emanuel Swedenborg, all against Sullivan's wishes. But she seems to have made no inquiries or efforts to learn about disabled professionals, disabled trades-people, or other adults with disabilities living on their own. She appears to have had no contact with the American Blind People's Higher Education and General Improvement Association, the turn-of-the-century network of blind professionals and intellectuals of her own generation who published the advocacy journal *The Problem*.[14] Nor did she link with the blind school alumni associations or with the next generation of organized blind activists, who formed state associations in the 1930s and the

National Federation of the Blind in 1940. After Sullivan's death in 1936, she continued in this pattern.

Keller's isolation not only contributed to her inability to successfully politicize disability as an issue of rights, prejudice, or discrimination, but also limited her actions. She neither experienced, nor saw herself as part of, a minority or oppressed group, only as an individual who had difficulties. Her oralist stance and opposition to the Deaf community's vigorous defense of American Sign Language is one example. Another example is that at the height of her involvement in radical politics, she supported eugenic and euthanasia policies to prevent the birth and sustenance of children with significant impairments. This position accorded with the eugenic thought of both radicals and conservatives of her era. In her latter years, unlike activists in the politicized groups of disabled people that existed during her lifetime, she never referred to discrimination against disabled people, or called for anti-discrimination laws, or went beyond legislative lobbying and fund-raising for AFB programs. The work programs she promoted were sheltered workshops condemned by the activist disability movements, and particularly by the organized blind movement, as exploitative and segregated. Whether or not she was aware of these criticisms is unclear. What is clear is that her highly public persona as a person with a disability limited not only her political options regarding disability issues but also the effectiveness of other advocates' attempts to define disability as a legitimate political category. Her visits to World War II veterans with disabilities show some acknowledgment of a parallel group experience, but the purpose of her visits was to inspire the veterans to personally "overcome" their disability. For her to have argued that blind people comprised a political category comparable to class, and that the myriad of disability experiences resulted in a shared political identity, would have been truly revolutionary.

Keller failed to move beyond her political individualism also because, like other disabled superstars, she became mired in the performance and ideology of perpetually overcoming her disability. This purpose isolated her from other people with disabilities, for it implied that she was stronger, braver, better, and more determined than they. It also implied that the responsibility for meeting legal, physical, or cultural barriers lay entirely on her shoulders, and that she should respond to such barriers with cheerfulness and vigor.[15] This strategic move allowed her to escape the role of a housebound invalid but depoliticized disability by relegating it to the realm of coping and personal character.

Initially, Keller tried to reject both the invalid and overcomer roles—not by confrontation, but by claiming the female role. This rejection did not work for her because no one saw her as "simply female," and because the female role itself implied a kind of "invalidism." Neither could she develop a public image comparable to that of Franklin Roosevelt—that of a disabled person who physically, psychologically, and morally triumphed, with courage and cheer, and by sheer individual will, over daily adversity and returned to *normal* social networks. Unlike Roosevelt, her disability *was* her public image, performance, and role—to remain in character, she kept continually "overcoming." Being blind and deaf was, as Anne Finger puts it, "her vocation." The novelty of her disability and the star status she achieved created for her a public space and voice.[16]

Though this may have been a lonely public space, it had the twisted and double-edged benefit of making Keller the mythological person she remains in the public imagination. That role provided her with financial benefits, international travel, public attention, and worldwide stardom. It enabled her to remain unique, garnering attention for both herself and Anne Sullivan. It created a career for the two of them when few were available to women and even fewer available to women with disabilities. An alliance with other people with disabilities would have destroyed her public image as a one-of-a-kind miracle. Given the limited practical or theoretical options perceptible to her, her isolation from other people with disabilities, and her inability to politicize disability, her career can be explained as a pragmatic choice. Few viable alternative choices existed.

Given Keller's early radicalism and political engagements, her failure to adapt radical or progressive analyses to the situation of blind people or others with disabilities is frustrating to the contemporary observer. At the center of this failure is the reality that most of what she acquired in life depended on—and had always depended on—her playing the *role* of Helen Keller. To adapt radical or progressive analyses to people with disabilities would have been the undoing of Keller as an individual performance and would have made her one of a social class. Anne Sullivan, Alexander Graham Bell, Perkins School for the Blind, and the American Foundation for the Blind all worked to construct the persona of Helen Keller, but Keller herself embraced and worked hard to maintain this public image. From the moment Sullivan entered her life, throughout her years as a child at Perkins, and throughout her years of national and international travel, she more or less consciously fashioned herself as a public figure whose public persona depended on—quite literally as well as figuratively—her marked *difference* and distance from others with a disability, as well as from those who considered themselves *able* and *normal*. This choice, however, helped to frustrate and, even after her death, would continue to frustrate the efforts of disability activists to make the theoretical and political moves that she found difficult.

This biography of Helen Keller relies on the analytical tools and scholarship of the emerging field of disability studies. This field moves away from a medical model of disability, which understands disability to be an individual pathology of the body that necessitates treatment. It also moves away from a sentimental cultural model of disability, which posits disability as a tragic affliction meriting pity, amazement, or seclusion. Instead, this approach examines how politics, culture, economics, and larger ideological notions of normality define who is and who is not disabled; or conversely, who is and who is not normal. It also reveals to historians, such as myself, the depth to which those definitions of disability and normality are ever-changing, are historically bound, and have immense consequence. Using disability as a tool of analysis necessitates a profound rethinking of power and the dynamics which create social power.[17]

Like many other women, Helen Keller sought to fully embrace the potential power of her citizenship in a society that considered her inadequate for citizenship. Unlike many other women, however, her supposed inadequacies included a disability. Other historians, biographers, and activists have argued effectively that race, class, religion, and sexual orientation intersect with gender to shape women's civic lives. Helen Keller's life illustrates that our physical bodies, and more important the ways those bodies are interpreted, also shape our civic lives.

This political biography is not simply entitled *The Radical Lives of Helen Keller* because of Keller's interest in radical politics. She also lived radically different lives at different points in her life. Internal and hard wrought personal decisions affected these changes. External factors, such as her college experience, the death of Anne Sullivan Macy, and laws and attitudes discriminating against people with disabilities also prompted these changes. *The Radical Lives of Helen Keller* seeks to recognize the various political lives Keller lived and the reasons for those political and personal revolutions.

1

I Do Not Like This
World As It Is

1900–1924

> I do not like this world as it is. I am trying to make it a lit-
> tle more as I would like to have it.   —Helen Keller, 1913

Anne Sullivan, Keller insisted, transformed her from "Phantom" to
"Helen." As an elderly woman she referred to her pre-Sullivan childhood
self as "'Phantom' . . . the little being governed only by animal impulses."[1]
She believed her teacher enabled her to become fully human by teaching
her language. It was the first major transformation in her life.

College similarly transformed Keller from a child to an adult. Many
considered her disability to mean that she would be forever childish and
childlike, regardless of age. She was never able to dismantle everyone's debilitating assumptions about her disability but graduating from Radcliffe
radically changed her own. Becoming an adult meant moving away from
the highly insulated life of a middle-class young girl made even more isolated by fame, deaf-blindness, an Alabama farm, and a Boston institution
for blind children. Becoming an adult meant moving away from Tuscumbia and Perkins, turning to teachers and a world beyond Sullivan,
wrestling with self-sufficiency on all levels, and embracing herself as fully
human. It is frustrating that most of our cultural memories of Helen
Keller end before she even got this far.

When Helen entered Radcliffe College in 1900 at twenty years of age,
she encountered a knot of conflicting messages. Radcliffe, the female
counterpart to Harvard, was one of the premier colleges for young women.

15

Geographically and metaphorically, it lay in the heart of Boston's long tradition of female political engagement and education. At the same time, the general debate about the moral, physical, and social advisability of a college education for young women echoed throughout its halls. Leading educators and physicians warned that the fragile bodies of young women would be masculinized, rendered sterile, or otherwise irreparably damaged by a higher education. The young women who risked a college degree struggled with these fears. As historian Douglas Baynton has pointed out, these warnings alleged that the female body itself was inherently disabled—the female brain, body, and mental state feeble and precarious.[2]

To enter college, Keller had not only to deal with her allegedly disabled female body but also the supposed failings of her actually disabled body. By the time she entered Radcliffe, she had endured nearly twenty years of deliberations as to whether or not she had the capacity to learn, to communicate, or simply to be "decent" in a public space. While to her, "the thought of going to college took root in my heart and became an earnest desire," to others her college admission was unadvisable, unnatural, and even dangerous. The skeptical interpreted any physical ailment of hers as evidence of a nervous and physical breakdown due to overwork, proof that her body was unable to withstand the rigors that college demanded of even the *normal* female body. Anne Sullivan, critics insisted, had to be the real brains and student of the duo, since surely Keller's disability rendered her incapable.[3]

Radcliffe thrilled and unsettled her. She mastered French, German, Greek, and Latin, but the structural impediments were huge. Few books were Brailled. Sullivan had to finger-spell most written materials and all course lectures, a time-consuming and physically taxing process for both of them. Sullivan's eyesight, which multiple surgeries had improved, now weakened seriously. Looking back in 1956, Keller remembered the agony caused by Sullivan's ailing eyes: "How I hated books at that moment! . . . When she asked if I did not want certain passages reread, I lied and declared that I could recall them." The measures taken by Radcliffe during examinations, intended to prevent Sullivan from giving Keller the answers, often included monitors unfamiliar with finger-spelling or Braille. This made difficult examinations almost overwhelming. In *The Story of My Life*, Keller attempted to dismiss the structural impediments, framing them, and her disability, as character building: "if they unintentionally placed obstacles in my way, I have the consolation of knowing that I overcame them all."[4]

Radcliffe was also personally isolating. Helen admitted, "I have sometimes had a depressing sense of isolation in the midst of my classmates." Few could communicate with her. She lived apart from the rest of the students and was already a celebrity. The academics were intellectually exciting and provocative: "My soul was set aflame!" Yet she grew frustrated at the failure of her professors to link course materials to contemporary and personal conditions: "Many scholars forget, it seems to me, that our enjoyment of the great works of literature depends more upon the depth of our sympathy than upon our understanding." This frustration may have deepened because of her passion for and dependence on the written word, which intensified while at Radcliffe. As she put it, "literature is my Utopia. Here I am not disfranchised. No barrier of the senses shuts me out from the sweet, gracious discourse of my book-friends."[5]

While her professors "seemed as impersonal as victrolas," and pals among her classmates were few, she developed intimate intellectual and personal friends among the students and young instructors at Harvard. These relationships shaped her views of the world. Sullivan remained at the center. John Macy was pivotal. At the recommendation of her friend Lenore Smith, he entered her realm to edit her best-selling *The Story of My Life* (1903) and stayed to marry Sullivan in 1905.[6]

To Anne and Helen, John Macy seemed a prize; or, as Helen later called him, "a friend, a brother, and an adviser all in one." The Harvard graduate with degrees in English and philosophy taught as a Harvard and Radcliffe instructor. Though on scholarship while earning his B.A., he had risen to become editor-in-chief of the *Harvard Advocate*, gained admittance into the best Harvard clubs, and was considered a rising writer, literary critic, and poet. He was tall and many believed him handsome. He wasn't wealthy, but both women thrilled to his vigorous conversation about literary and public affairs. Activists like John Reed and Arturo Giovannitti considered the socialist a friend. Anne was eleven years older; Helen three years younger. Once hired as Helen's editor, he quickly learned the manual alphabet and expanded his duties to serve as her publishing agent. Both women enjoyed his company, though his and Anne's courtship was always tumultuous.[7]

A couple who shared a boarding house with Macy, Harvard geology student Philip Smith and his wife Lenore, also became fast friends, Lenore even more because she could finger-spell proficiently. Twenty-five years later, Keller fondly remembered the popcorn and cider-filled evenings of Boston's winters as pivotal to her political and personal development. These experiences cemented her conviction, as she indicated in a 1913 *New York Times* article, that she did not "like this world as it is," but that she should try "to make it a little more as I would like to have it."

> Many times during the long winter evenings we sat around an open fire with a circle of eager, imaginative students, drinking cider, popping corn, and joyously tearing to pieces society, philosophies, religions, and literatures. . . . We believed in the rising tide of the masses, in peace, in brotherhood, and "a square deal" for everybody. Each of us had an idol around whom our theories revolved like planets around the sun. These idols had familiar names—Nietzsche, Schopenhauer, Karl Marx, Bergson, Lincoln, Tolstoi, and Max Stirner. The more we read and discussed, the more convinced we were that we belonged to that choice coterie who rise in each age, and manage to attain freedom of thought. . . . And the endless discussions that darkened counsel! For each of us had a panacea to turn this barren world into a paradise, and each defended his special kingdom with argument flashed against argument in true dueling fashion.[8]

The discussions invigorated her, the readings provoked, but what may have been most intellectually and politically emancipating to her was philosophy. Descartes' maxim, "I think, therefore I am," reinforced her internally tenuous claim that she was completely human. "They waked," she wrote in 1929, "something in me that has never slept since." Because she could think, her perceptions, analyses, and senses of the world were legitimate. Though she was deaf and blind, she could metaphorically and literally read the world accurately. Such a claim, legitimated by the paragons of Western philosophical thought, was revolutionary to the young woman.[9]

Having friends was also revolutionary. She had fun. Never before, at home in Tuscumbia or in Boston at Perkins, had she developed intimate friendships outside of Anne Sullivan (with whom she was still in the process of becoming a compatriot rather than a pupil). Keller was never an integral part of the intimate and emotional network of early twentieth-century female reformers, but while at Radcliffe she learned that she could have friends. It was thrilling.

Literary success also revolutionized Keller's world. *The Story of My Life* (1903) became an almost unparalleled best seller in many languages. The autobiography (as much as one can write a life story at twenty-three years of age!) enhanced her international reputation and that of Anne Sullivan. With this, she dreamt of almost unlimited opportunities and of life as an economically self-sufficient author.

While in college, in the midst of these new experiences, she wrestled seriously with issues of money, vocation, and work. She had to choose and grasp one of those unlimited opportunities. She faced a question familiar to many: "What are you going to do when you graduate from college?" For her, however, this question was profoundly complicated. It was 1903—she was female, and she was a person with a significant disability. For these reasons, many believed she shouldn't have been educated in the first place; and for these reasons, wage employment was difficult to secure. In a *Ladies Home Journal* essay entitled "My Future as I See It," she acknowledged her disability but imagined her future and justified her education in terms similar to those used by other college educated women of her generation. Like Jane Addams, for example, she sought to be useful, and to use her education, but felt the very real constraints of being female. She emphasized a distinctly female form of service, rather than personal ambition, and never mentioned the need for a wage: "Opportunities to be of service to others offer themselves constantly, and every day, every hour, calls even on me for a timely word of action. It bewilders me to think of the countless tasks that may be mine." In 1905, she called upon all "college girls" to embrace this "spirit of service." For her, service included studying economic questions related to women and their advancement, advocating for deaf and blind people, writing, translating, adopting and then teaching a deaf child, fund-raising for "good causes," caring for the sick, or engaging in settlement house work (a common form of work for college-educated women of her generation).[10]

Service mattered to Helen also for religious reasons. In 1896, she had converted to Swedenborgianism, a Christian group established by the Swedish spiritual leader Emanuel Swedenborg and a growing movement among turn-of-the-century Americans. Samuel Gridley Howe had attempted to use his deaf-blind student Laura Bridgman as a religious experiment, unsuccessfully denying her religious teachings in hopes that she would develop her own sense of God, thus proving that human beings were guided by "innate religious intuitions."[11] Anagnos had attempted to do the same with the young Helen, also unsuccessfully. For both men, denying the young girls any religious teaching proved impossible. Bridgman became an evangelical Baptist. Helen gained faith from the teachings of Swedenborg given to her in Braille by Alexander Graham Bell's secretary John Hitz.

Helen came to Swedenborgianism despite the lack of enthusiasm from Anne, who cared little about religious matters, or from her family, who were Presbyterians and Episcopalians. The Swedenborgian belief in "the separateness between soul and body" thrilled her. Swedenborg taught that there was a "spiritual body within the material one with perfect senses" that mattered more than the material body. Thus, her deaf-blindness mattered little. In fact, because Swedenborg believed that the "matter-clogged, mirage-filled senses"[12] sometimes kept the faithful from the spiritual senses that enabled them to know God, Helen believed her disability may have made possible a *deeper* sense of spirituality that would open to her "a world infinitely more wonderful, complete, and satisfying than this one." Everyone had the potential to access that world, according to Swedenborg, both before and after death.[13] While others interpreted her disability as debilitating, Keller's faith tradition interpreted her disability as a possible spiritual bonus. Today many people with disabilities embrace theologies that similarly reject the importance of the physical body and emphasize the importance of a spiritual body.

As Helen later wrote in 1928, "Swedenborg says that 'the perfection of man is the love of use,' or service to others." She acknowledged that her deaf-blindness could make her service "limited," but found the teachings of Swedenborg deeply satisfying because they emphasized that living a "life of the spirit" was enough. Swedenborg guaranteed to her that physical impairments did not impair her spiritual life. Living the "life of the spirit" gave to all love, which provided "release from the evils of physical and mental blindness." As long as her will to service was strong, Swedenborg assured her that her service would come.[14] The Swedenborgian tradition thus not only satisfied her spiritually, but also its emphasis on service provided impetus and justification for her political sentiments and actions.

Though her will for service was strong, and though she believed service would come, service was frustrating. The list of options was shorter than she had imagined. In the years following her college graduation, she wrote: "the avenues of usefulness open to me were not many, and even while I stood debating which I should follow I found that I had no choice in the matter."[15]

Upon her college graduation in 1904, Keller imagined her most viable and important public role to be advocacy for deaf and blind people. She already had addressed both the Massachusetts and New York legislatures on behalf of bills funding manual training for blind people. She felt that with additional education she could accomplish great things: "If these workers and philanthropists in Massachusetts and New York thought that I, a junior in college, could help hundreds of unfortunate men and women, how much greater must my chances of usefulness be when I comprehend more fully the needs of the deaf and blind! . . . I must follow where the good cause leads." These efforts constituted lobbying, but they differed from her later efforts that were organized and initiated by the American Foundation for the Blind. These pre-AFB activities sat ideologically and organizationally on the edge of the large-scale social reform networks of progressive and radical women who sought to transform the nation and the world.[16]

The "good cause" also led to fund-raising. Keller's first appeals were intensely emotional and echoed earlier fund-raising displays of Perkins students by Samuel Gridley Howe.[17] Just a recent college graduate, she sought money for existing institutions such as the New York Eye and Ear Infirmary and the New York Association for the Blind. She emphasized the responsibility of the able-bodied to give: it was "a sacred burden," a "blessing to the strong to give help to the weak." At most events she was the featured attraction. As Alexander Graham Bell or Sullivan relayed her words, crowds stared at her through lorgnettes (similar to opera glasses). According to the *New York Times*, women cried and men "coughed uneasily." Keller's appeal—"I do not wish to be a beggar, but I hope this basket will be filled with checks"—filled the basket repeatedly.[18]

These early events in Keller's public life reflect the changing nature of reform and benevolence in the United States. The events uneasily emphasized both pity for and the potential independence of people with disabilities. She and others appealed to the public's sympathy and lamented disability as an unfortunate tragedy. Tears flowed, as she conveyed "an infinity of pathos." At the same time she and her colleagues formed a "comparatively new movement" that sought economic and personal self-sufficiency for people who were blind, "practical" assistance that was distinctly not charity and that fostered independence. Using this argument, she grew more confident in her fund-raising abilities. By 1913, she could say easily, "I am shameless in my begging." Meanwhile, as institutions for people with disabilities became more professionalized, and as reform became an increasingly female profession, she moved from emphasizing the emotion of the giver and the suffering of the recipient to the potential self-sufficiency of the recipient. This was a major transition.[19]

The good cause also led in unexpected directions. Keller spoke of the scandalous and taboo, advocated federal intervention in health services and education, and indicted capitalism. Reading and research had taught her, she said, that blindness, deafness, tuberculosis and "other causes of suffering" were not simply uncontrollable forces of nature that needed to be borne with "as much fortitude as we could gather": "Those evils are to be laid not at the door of Providence, but at the door of mankind; that they are, in large measure, due to ignorance, stupidity and sin." Because ignorance, stupidity, and sin were involved, action was necessary.[20]

In the first decade of the century, at least two-fifths of all blindness in the United States was due to *opthalmia neonatorum*, a highly treatable infection of newborns caused by the mother's venereal disease. Because of what Keller called "false modesty—the shame that shelters evil," few doctors, public health officials, or legislators were willing to confront, much less discuss, the issue. This refusal infuriated her. She acknowledged in a 1909 *Ladies Home Journal* article that "the subject was one of which a young woman [such as herself] might be supposed to be ignorant," but called for all American women (as well as churches, schools, and the press) to demand that federal funds and education ensure that all children received the cheap preventive eye-drops at birth.[21]

Ladies Home Journal editor Edward Bok was praised for his publishing courage, but Keller's 1909 article had conservative elements. She blamed "licentious men" entirely for the spread of venereal disease. She explained women's infection by stating that "previous to the child's birth she has unconsciously received it through infection from her husband. He has contracted the infection in licentious relations before or since marriage." Looking back in 1938, she referred to the forthrightness of this article with pride.[22]

On a much deeper level, however, by 1910, Keller's study of blindness contributed to her indictment of capitalism. What she had previously considered to be the glories and logic of industrial progress became, in her new analysis, the cause of great harm: industrial accidents, economic inequality, poverty, inadequate nutrition, and inadequate or nonexistent healthcare. Schools for the blind were not enough. Nor were eye-drops: "Our worst foes are ignorance, poverty, and the unconscious cruelty of our commercial society. These are the causes of blindness; these are the enemies that destroy the sight of children and workmen and undermine the health of mankind. So long as these enemies remain unvanquished, so long will there be blind and crippled men and women." She also began to recognize the power of privilege. Education, class, race, and connections had helped her to achieve, but "the power to rise in the world is not within the reach of everyone." The task of advocating for deaf and blind people thus went far beyond her previous expectations. It demanded a major transformation of society. There was a connection, she insisted, between "our prosperity and the sorrows of others."[23]

As a consequence of this intellectual and political shift, beginning in the late 1900s and continuing through the early 1920s, Keller joined the large, growing number of increasingly mainstream Americans involved in radical and progressive politics. Because she was one of the most famous and recognizable women in the world, all that she did commanded attention. Her involvement included public speaking tours, published articles, appearances at rallies and congressional hearings, friendships and correspondence with other activists, and membership in organizations such as the American Civil Liberties Union. Her writings, public presentations, and private correspondence reflect wide-ranging interests and wide-ranging knowledge but centered on class issues.

Keller joined the Socialist Party in 1909, part of what her biographer Joseph Lash called the "intellectual earthquake" that shook her household that year. First, John Macy, who by then was married to Anne Sullivan, joined the Socialist Party. Helen soon followed, like thousands of workers, intellectuals, farmers, wealthy, and indigent, inspired by the compelling leadership of Socialist Party President Eugene V. Debs. When explaining how she became a socialist, she said, "By reading," and cited the "book-friend" H. G. Wells's *New Worlds for Old*. Theories of social and individual progress attracted her. Like virtually all college women of her generation, she put great faith in the redeeming power of social science and logic.

Wells's explanation of socialism as "a great intellectual process" resulting in "a project for the reshaping of human society upon new and better lines" appealed to her faith in intellect and human effort. And she was a good socialist. After reading one of her essays, Industrial Workers of the World (IWW) strike organizer and hero, Arturo Giovannitti, a close friend of John Macy, praised her. "She has grasped the full meaning of the socialist movement as well as any grizzled strategos of the class war," he said, " . . . *none of us will contend any more that she does not deserve to go to jail* (italics added)."[24]

These were rousing years for Helen. She had interesting and provocative friends, and she saw a bright and varied future for herself. Anne, now Mrs. Macy, was at her happiest, and Helen loved living at Wrentham with her and John. Next to Anne, she described him as "the friend who discovered most ways to give me pleasure and gratify my intellectual curiosity." The relationship between Anne and Helen was transforming from that of teacher and pupil to one of genuine friendship. Looking back in 1956, Helen wrote that marriage brought "a welcome change" to Anne and their relationship. "Her fingers—not to say her tongue—were loosed, and I thrilled to a new kind of companionship. In a home of our own, whenever John read aloud to us about controversial questions, Teacher spelled her opinions to me without reserve, and it was both entertaining and amusing for her and me to quarrel comfortably." Her 1929 biography *Midstream* describes this period as pastoral but busy, full of pets, plants, farm buildings, changing seasons, lectures, and never enough time to do dishes. "Small events were full of poetry, and the glory of the spirit lay over all."[25]

The years were also productive. Again with John Macy's assistance as editor, agent, and friend, Keller published *The World I Live In* (1908) and *The Song of the Stone Wall* (1910). "I do not remember," Keller wrote later, "writing anything in such a happy mood as *The World I Live In*." The book continued her rebuttal of those who thought her incapable of intelligent perception by explaining how taste, touch, and smell created a rich sensory world. *The Song of the Stone Wall* is an example of her perception, using poetry to convey the long stone wall near the Wrentham home.[26]

Portrait of Helen Keller, John Macy, and Anne Sullivan Macy, undated. *Courtesy of the American Foundation for the Blind. Used with permission of the American Foundation for the Blind, Helen Keller Archives.*

Politics took up the rest of the time. Keller subscribed to a German socialist periodical printed in Braille, hung a large red flag in her study, routinely read the *International Socialist Review*, and involved herself increasingly in socialist issues. When Fred Warren, editor of the socialist newspaper *Appeal to Reason* was arrested for sending "scurrilous, defamatory and threatening" literature through the mail, she protested his "unrighteous conviction."[27] When the party battled over tactics in 1913, she issued a public call for harmony, scolding members: "Are we to put difference of party tactics before the desperate needs of the workers? . . . Shame on us! The enemy is at our very doors, and the hand of the destroyer does its fell work, while we leave the victims helpless." She supported the faltering socialist paper the New York *Call* with $50 worth of bonds as well as humor, warning the paper that "I hope the whole stock-bond, rent-interest-and-profit system is out of business before they fall due."[28] She also publicly supported socialist leaders and candidates—IWW strike leader Arturo Giovannitti in 1914, New York mayoral candidate Morris Hillquit in 1917, and the arrested Eugene Debs in 1919. During her travels she sought local political "comrades," telling John Macy that they greeted her "warmly" wherever she went. In 1914, she joined the Los Angeles Local of the Socialist Party.[29]

Poverty and the unequal distribution of resources pained her greatly. Education, literature, travel, social debates, and meeting many different kinds of people wonderfully expanded her world. But she struggled with the incongruities: "the bright world of my imagining" did not live up to the "world of facts—a world of misery and degradation, of blindness, crookedness, and sin, a world struggling against the elements, against the unknown, against itself." Those who labored most harshly, who suffered most profoundly because of labor, then benefited little from that labor. "We cannot," she insisted, "shut our eyes to these glaring evils. . . . I am the determined foe of the capitalist system, which denies the workers the rights of human beings. I consider it fundamentally wrong, radically unjust and cruel."[30]

When workers struck, Keller quickly supported them. Through strike activism she became involved with the radical union Industrial Workers of the World (IWW or "Wobblies"). The IWW sought to unite all workers, skilled and unskilled, in the overthrow of capitalism via strikes, direct action, propaganda, and boycotts. During World War I, the Wobblies opposed military service because they considered the war a profit-making venture for already-wealthy industrialists. Inspired by the massive and successful IWW strike in Lawrence, Massachusetts, she joined 1912 strike efforts in Little Falls, Massachusetts, by sending a letter of encouragement and $87 to striking workers. John Macy read aloud the message at a strike meeting while strike leader Big Bill Haywood praised her actions. Keller called the cause of the strikers, 70 percent of them female, "my cause. If they are denied a living wage, I also am denied. While they are industrial slaves, I cannot be free."[31]

Both the radical and mainstream press showered attention on both her sentiments and her actions. In 1916, she explained that she had turned to the radical IWW because "the Socialist party was too slow. It is sinking in a political bog." It risked its "revolutionary character" by relying on electoral politics.[32] Echoing the famous phrase with which Karl Marx ended the *Communist Manifesto* she declared: "The worker has nothing to lose but his chains, and he has a whole world to win."[33]

Keller's political analysis grew from a belief in the centrality of class, but money and class held an uneasy place in her life. Like many other southern landholding whites, her father considered his family part of the upper class and benefited greatly from the privileges of class. Her family, however, had relatively few financial resources after the Civil War. Because of this she had depended on wealthy philanthropists to fund her education and daily needs. As an adult she found that making a living adequate for herself, Anne Macy (and later Polly Thomson) was difficult. Though an international figure, financial security remained a lifelong concern.

Keller believed work essential for herself and other people with disabilities, though she focused almost exclusively on blind people, if they were to advance personally and as a group. The lack of wage work, she argued, resulted in a "bondage of idleness and despair," "a state of idleness more terrible even than loss of sight." It produced "idle, dependent lives."[34] Wage work would bring economic and personal independence. Work would "raise the sightless of America from isolation and idleness to a useful citizenship and some measure of happiness"; it would "help the blind to help themselves." "Work and happiness," she wrote, "go hand in hand." In 1924, she argued that the "idle adult blind" were "a public or a private burden, a bad debt, an object of pitying charity, and an economic loss." Work was the salvation. Work would raise blind people from "dependence to self-respecting citizenship" and allow them to become "useful blind people."[35]

Therefore, Keller advocated that private organizations, state governments, and other civic entities could best help blind people by establishing employment agencies and work training programs. She suggested that state agencies encourage the public to employ blind individuals as "piano tuners, notepaper embossers, shampooers, masseurs, chairmakers, brushmakers, tutors, singers, church organists, tea tasters." Blind people, she said, could manufacture mattresses and brooms; perform simple carpentry and weaving; work at massage, typewriting, knitting and crocheting, and traveling sales; raise poultry; and operate small businesses such as newsstands and tobacco and candy shops. She repeated versions of this message in public addresses before state and national legislatures, women's reform organizations, and organizations focused on blind people.[36]

These types of activities placed Keller within a lineage of educators, activists, and reformers, who had sought employment for people with disabilities, even though major differences existed in this lineage. In the nineteenth century, Samuel Gridley Howe, founder of Perkins School for the Blind, initially sought manual training for blind people to make them economically competitive rather than dependent receivers of charity. Eventually he acquiesced to the larger cultural assumption, as described by historian Mary Klages, that "the blind body [was] an unsuitable site for competitive labor in the context of industrial production." Historians have shown that some people with disabilities organized themselves to reject explicitly the notion that disability implied economic dependence and idleness. Deaf leaders from the 1880s through the late 1940s sought expanded employment opportunities for Deaf workers and challenged anti–deaf discrimination. The League of the Physically Handicapped protested employment discrimination in work-relief agencies and the Works Progress Administration (WPA) during the Depression. Each of these groups used the language of rights and discrimination, not charity.[37]

Keller's advocacy of paid employment is contradictory, even if one recognizes the changes in her tone and emphasis throughout her lifetime. She acknowledged employment discrimination against people with disabilities. The solution she sought, however, was not a confrontation with discrimination but the creation of segregated work opportunities for people with disabilities. In 1907, she wrote, "even the educated, industrious blind cannot earn their living without more special assistance than they now receive" because the employing public "often does not believe that they can work." In this case, she highlighted discrimination; but her solution was to establish segregated work opportunities for the blind—what are now referred to as "sheltered workshops." Such efforts may have created work opportunities for blind people, but because they emphasized the isolation and *difference* of people with disabilities, many of the organized blind and deaf people opposed them.[38]

Keller considered work essential because it meant economic autonomy. Though much of the public considered people with disabilities "proper paupers," she knew that being an object of charity, even a proper one, "cast [one] out of the public economic realm into the private sphere of charity."[39] Besides leaving that economic realm, one also then left the civic realm and the civic legitimacy so important to her. She recognized that idleness (as she characterized the lack of wage work) was not a privilege for people with disabilities but a highly stigmatized status that undermined social legitimacy and cast people with disabilities as second-class citizens. This reality was reflected in nineteenth- and twentieth-century immigration restrictions that denied entry to individuals with bodies judged unable to earn a living.[40]

Adopting and reinforcing the culturally dominant assumption of a relationship between paid employment and civic and moral worth placed Keller in several quandaries at once. The distinction she drew between a useful and a dependent citizenry implied that unless and until blind people (those she referred to most often) engaged in paid work, they were not and could not be good citizens. But employers, social welfare policies, and often educational institutions defined people with disabilities as incapable of productive work. That rendered the vast majority incapable of good citizenship.

This dichotomy also undermined Keller's own claims to moral and civic virtue because she was not as economically self-sufficient as she desired and claimed to be. She used work to distinguish herself from the many unemployed people with disabilities, devalued by society as unproductive and dependent. In 1904, still wrestling with postcollege graduation panic, she insisted that she had found "abundant work" and that it was a "blessedness." The publication of *The Story of My Life* in 1903 was a success and she considered herself a professional writer. Yet the money she earned was not enough to support her household in the fashion she desired, so she depended on the philanthropy of the wealthy. She wanted to write on subjects other than her own disability, but editors tended to be uninterested. Money was a constant stress. Helen Keller was, in fact, not economically independent. Her claims to the economic independence she thought essential for civic and moral worth were tenuous at best.[41]

Keller's embrace of the culturally dominant assumption that paid employment and civic virtue were linked was also awkward because of the tangled knot of gender, race, class status, and disability she embodied. Asserting that she was a good and useful citizen because she earned money was not a simple claim. In the framework of turn-of-the-century citizenship, productive and self-supporting work made men good civic agents. But able-bodied, middle-class white women achieved civic virtue via economic and social *dependency* on a husband or father. On the other hand, for able-bodied black and poor white women, dependency marked a problem to be *fixed* by work. For women with disabilities, regardless of color, dependency exaggerated and contributed to the interpretation of their disability as debilitating.[42]

Linking her wage-earning to civic virtue might have aided Keller as an individual, but it reinforced her status as aberrant, in terms of her gender and class background. It also distanced her from other people with disabilities. Furthermore, when she listed possible occupations for people with disabilities, she generally listed male trade occupations. What were women with disabilities to do? Women with disabilities found wage work virtually impossible to secure. Their claims for legitimacy were complicated not only by their gender, and sometimes by their race, but also by the limited employment possibilities and social stigma encountered by many people with disabilities.

Some able-bodied women used actual or metaphorical maternalism to claim good citizenship. Motherhood or the potential for motherhood, they insisted, rendered them uniquely qualified to care for the nation or the world. This claim too, however, was unavailable to many women with disabilities, because of the belief that they could not and should not bear children.

Keller's intellectual, political, and personal wrestling with the meanings of work reveal the challenge that the disabled body, as well the gendered body, presents to democratic societies. Democratic societies are founded on the premise that autonomy and independence are neutral concepts equally attainable by everyone. Keller tried to argue, in various ways throughout her life, that people with disabilities could work and that impairment did not necessarily imply moral and civic disability. In this case, however, that was fiction. She was stuck because she failed to question the myth that everyone—regardless of body, race, or gender—had equal and lifelong access to wage work. Despite her interest in radical politics, her concern for class inequalities, and her awareness of gender inequalities, she was unable to challenge the fiction that autonomy and independence were there for all. Autonomy and independence were all she wanted.

Throughout these years of analyzing U.S. politics, Keller still had to confront the reality that she couldn't support herself or her household adequately. When Andrew Carnegie offered her a regular pension income in 1910, she turned him down. Perhaps she was uneasy accepting cash from one of the nation's wealthiest industrialists while she attacked capitalism. Perhaps she was uneasy with the dependence and all it might demand. She had joined the Socialist Party the year before and increasingly targeted capitalism. She wrote to Carnegie that she needed to make it on her own and hoped that the (in)famously self-made man would understand.

> I realize that a large sum of money would broaden my work and increase my pleasures. But my kind friends have given me the necessary equipment—education, books and a house to live in. I lack no essential comfort . . . I hope to enlarge my life and work by my own efforts, and you, sir, who have won prosperity from small beginnings will uphold me in

my decision to fight my battles without further help than I am now receiving from loyal friends and a generous world. . . . My joys and sorrows are bound up indissolubly with the joys and sorrows of my fellowmen, and I feel far more blessed to see them receiving new opportunities, better tools with which to do their work, than I could feel if I received more for myself when I already have a fair share, and millions have less than their rightful portion.[43]

Money matters, however, did not disappear and 1913 was a difficult year. Keller found it "a marvel" to live with her two fiercest critics—the married John and Anne—to aid her in putting together a collection of political and social commentaries. But *Out of the Dark* made little money. Panning the book, critics questioned her ability to develop valid social observations on her own. According to her later literary agent, Nella Braddy Henney, at this point Keller gave up hope of supporting herself with literary works.[44] On top of everything else, the Macy marriage was collapsing and John fled to Europe.

In April 1913, Helen wrote to Carnegie again. The week before Anne had taken severely ill in a hotel while the two were traveling. Eventually, Anne gathered enough strength, but meanwhile Helen had been unable to summon help. Helen described the experience as "disconcerting," "an overpowering sense of my helplessness came over me." Remembering Carnegie's promise that he and his wife would always help if needed, she accepted his offer. "I was ambitious," she wrote to Carnegie, "to earn my own living and to make things easier for those that I love. But I did not understand until now that in order to carry out this idea I should have to lay another burden upon the dear shoulders of those who were already heavily burdened."[45] Only months earlier Carnegie had asked her it if was true that she had become a socialist. When she admitted it, he threatened to lay the thirty-three-year-old woman across his knees and spank her if she did not come to "her senses."[46] She received a Carnegie pension for decades but never wrote about her feelings on the matter.

The need for money created a consistent tension between Keller's economic reliance on philanthropists and her personal desire for independence. Though she largely solicited for others rather than herself, tension also always remained between her lifelong appeals to wealthy philanthropists and her political critiques of capitalism. Her disability made class security slippery, so did her gender and Anne Macy's. By this point in their lives neither could rely on a husband for money. Her political analysis included a critique of the poverty that accompanied capitalism, but she left no record of analyzing her own tenuous economic stance and the reasons for it.

Helen's personal struggles with economic independence and her political identity occurred simultaneously with major household transitions. In 1914, John and Anne separated permanently. It was a lengthy process of counteraccusations that Helen characterized as Anne's "greatest sorrow." Understandably, no one dealt well with the locked rooms, tears, and innumerable letters, accusations, and counteraccusations flying among the *three* of them. Everything about the situation pained Helen. Anne, Helen wrote, wept "as only women who are no longer cherished weep."[47] The lengthy and convoluted letters Helen wrote to John, in which she referred to his marriage to Anne while speaking fondly of the days in which "*we three* [italics added] seemed to feel in each other's handclasp a bit of heaven," probably did not help.[48] Additionally, financing and carrying out the daily activities of the household was proving difficult, and John's absence made it worse. Subsidized by the wealthy, Helen and Anne hired Polly Thomson, a Scottish immigrant, to help bring order to their lives and their household. The young woman knew no finger-spelling and had never even heard of the famous pair.

From 1913 on through 1920, Keller and Anne Macy traveled almost constantly. Sometimes Polly Thomson joined them, at other times they were accompanied by Keller's mother. Keller admitted that discovering everyone knew of her was "pleasant," but that "it was hard to accustom myself to the strangeness of public life." Back and forth across the continent they went. Keller claimed later that she could tell cities apart, and differentiate parts of cities, by their odor.[49]

In these years Keller tried to apply her political analysis to the status of women, arguing that women's rights were part of the larger issue of social justice for everyone. Perhaps it was also part of an effort to make sense of her and Anne Macy's life. As with the rest of her political views, the inequalities of class permeated her analysis. For example, just as in 1911, she was "indignant" at the imprisonment and forced feeding of British suffragists, so was she "indignant when the women cloakmakers of Chicago are abused by the police." The economic, political, and social tyranny of a few, she reasoned, caused both "indignities." When she declared herself a "militant suffragette" in 1913, she explained she did so because she believed female suffrage would lead to socialism.[50] When she endorsed birth control and the controversial advocate Margaret Sanger, she did so not in terms of women's bodily autonomy but in terms of the protection of the poor: "Only by taking the responsibility of birth control into their own hands can they roll back the awful tide of misery that is sweeping over them and their children."[51]

Like many female activists in the early part of the twentieth century, Keller argued for extending traditional female responsibilities into the larger world. The home, she insisted, was no longer a "private factory" but was explicitly linked to the larger capitalist market. Where women once made their own bread and butter, a thousand hands contributed to the bread and butter they now bought. Just as household members now had to leave the physical space of home to work at and buy from industrial businesses, so was the waste and illness wrought by industrial businesses brought back to the home. "Woman's place is still in the household," she conceded, "but the household is more spacious than in times gone by." Thus, women needed the vote; and the civic world needed the "mother spirit."[52]

Not all women, however, agreed on the implications of the "mother spirit." To today's reader, one of Keller's most disturbing contributions to public debate on poverty, gender, and disability regards eugenics, specifically the Bollinger baby case. In 1915, Dr. Harry Haiselden refused to perform a potentially life-saving operation on a Chicago infant, "the deformed Bollinger baby." The baby died. For Haiselden, it was a matter of eugenics: the belief that traits such as morality, intelligence, poverty, and wealth were hereditary and manifested on the body. The Bollinger baby, whom he believed had little if any mental capacity, was not worth treating for reasons of utility and eugenics. What use was the baby's life, he asked? He explained further, "The average physician today saves imbeciles at birth. This adds to the crime wave of the city's future."[53] The case became a national media event, and activists across the political spectrum, including many in the socialist and progressive movements, defended Haiselden. For some, their support lay in a deeply held faith in improvement and in the objectivity and intervention of experts. Applying this to human beings, they supported Haiselden and his effort to improve human genetics. The New York *Call*, a leading socialist paper, defended Haiselden in eugenic and class terms (but never examined the links between poverty and disability). Some writers ridiculed those who defended "defective" infants while ignoring those "crippled" by poverty.[54]

Keller figured into the Bollinger/Haiselden debate as a symbol and as an activist. In a widely reprinted critique of Haiselden, Jane Addams argued that "defectives" had made many great contributions to the world. As historian Martin Pernick explains, "Her honor roll of the 'world's great defectives' included Helen Keller, Charles Steinmetz, John Milton, and Talleyrand." Keller served as a symbol, easily understood by everyone, of the possible value to society of those considered defective.[55]

Keller herself entered the debate by endorsing Haiselden's actions. On the pages of the socialist New York *Call* (where she was a frequent contributor during this period) and the *New Republic*, she argued that the life of this baby and many others was "not worth while" and that many "hopeless death-in-life" cases existed. She called for a jury of physicians to decide on the life and death of any "idiot malformed baby." "A mental defective," she

wrote, "is almost sure to be a potential criminal." These were difficult issues, she acknowledged, but society must choose between "a fine humanity
like Dr. Haiselden's and a cowardly sentimentalism."[56]

In her adoption of eugenic sentiments Keller certainly failed to consider
her own life and its implications. *She* had once been considered to live a
"hopeless death-in-life." She may have distinguished between her "normality" at birth and the Bollinger baby's disability. The implications of eugenic thought, however, were the same regardless of when one acquired a
disability.

In the midst of the Haiselden/Bollinger baby debate, Keller also spoke
against the growing war in Europe. She drew the attention of automaker
Henry Ford, who entered the antiwar fray in November 1915. Ford char-
tered a ship that was to leave in one week—with 125 first-class cabins, 125
second, and 450 third-class cabins—to sail U.S. pacifists, socialists, antimil-
itarists, and other leaders to Europe in order to "stop the war." He invited
Jane Addams, famed journalist Ida Tarbell, Thomas Edison, all the state
governors, many business and religious leaders, and Helen Keller on the
six-week journey.[57] Keller declined, citing previously booked speaking engagements, but wrote eloquently and at length about the ugliness of war.[58]
Privately, she voiced her uncertainty about the effort and her decision: "I
wish I were on board the Peace Ship, it would be a most interesting adventure." Ford sought to reach the men in the trenches in order to convince
them of the futility of war. She realistically wondered how he would reach
and persuade them.[59]

In the decades before and after World War I, women led international
peace efforts, justifying their efforts with essentialist statements about
women's compassionate, peaceful, and benevolent nature. Keller was part
of this intellectual and political wave, and like some others included an
analysis of class. She encouraged the purchase of war bonds once World
War I began, but like the IWW she continually criticized the war as a
profit-making venture for military industrialists.[60] The workers, she said,
"suffer all the miseries [of war], while the rulers reap the rewards." She

warned a 1915 crowd of 2,000 cheering socialists that the army had "already proved itself an enemy of liberty" by involvement in strike breaking and urged working men to "destroy the war of the trenches." The war brought an immensely busy lecture schedule.[61]

Keller's analysis of Ford's possible effectiveness reflects her understanding of the war as one in which working peoples from enemy countries fought one another in the name of patriotism, while all suffered at the hands of capitalism.

> I wonder if Mr. Ford realizes what would be the consequences if the workers in the trenches united against a continuation of war. Of course he must. He is a practical man. . . . Would it not threaten all authority? Would it not give the world to the workers? In other words, if the men who are now in the trenches united to throw down the weapons which governments have put into their hands, and succeeded in this master stroke, that is, without being branded as cowards or shot as traitors, would they not use the same method to put an end to the industrial warfare of the world?[62]

She understood that hierarchies of power depended on one another for sustenance. When one was threatened, so were the others.

Keller attracted further political attention with a February 1916 $100 check to the National Association for the Advancement of Colored People. To NAACP Vice President Oswald Garrison Villard, she wrote:

> I warmly endorse your efforts to bring before the country the facts about the unfair treatment of the colored people in some parts of the United States. What a comment upon our social justice is the need of an association like yours! It should bring a blush of shame to the face of every true American to know that ten million of his countrymen are denied the equal protection of the laws. . . . *Ashamed in my very soul I behold in my own beloved south-land* the tears of those who are oppressed, those who must bring up their sons and daughters in bondage to be servants, be-

cause others have their fields and vineyards, and on the side of the op-
pressor is power. (italics added)

She used God to establish her authority. "The outrages against the colored people," she wrote, "are a denial of Christ."[63]

She sincerely believed this, but her sentiments also asserted her independence and inflamed her family. Activist W. E. B. Du Bois printed the letter in the NAACP's newspaper *The Crisis*. *The Selma* (Alabama) *Journal* also printed the letter and an accompanying editorial that described it as "full of untruths, full of fawning and bootlicking phrases." The editorial implied that Keller could not have formulated the sentiments herself: "The people who did such wonderful work in training Miss Keller must have belonged to the old Abolition Gang for they seemed to have thoroughly poisoned her mind against her own people."[64]

Pressured by her family, especially her mother's remonstrances about her extended family residing in Selma, Keller replied with a letter to the *Selma Times*. Her adult relationship with her mother reflected her concerns about her southern upbringing. In 1929, she wrote: "My mother talked intelligently, brilliantly, about current events, and she had a Southerner's interest in politics. . . . But after my mind had taken a radical turn she could never get over the feeling that we had drifted apart. It grieves me that I should have added to the sadness that weighed upon her." Keller's reply to the Selma newspaper claimed, with confused phrasing, that her original letter had advocated "equality of all men before the law," rather than "the social equality of white people and Negroes" that *The Selma Journal* editorial had implied. An anonymous letter in the *Selma Times* defended her, saying that she had been wrongfully charged with "statements of disloyalty to the South and to the integrity of Southern institutions."[65]

Simultaneous to the storm about Keller's NAACP letter, Anne Macy suffered ill health, made worse by the continued marital discord and a relatively unsuccessful 1916 Chautauqua tour for the student and teacher duo. Doctors advised her rest, which she took alone in Lake Placid, New York, and then Puerto Rico. With Macy gone, Helen planned to spend several months with her widowed mother in Alabama, perhaps smoothing over their relationship. Before leaving, however, she fell in love.

By falling in love, Helen personally ran up against eugenic sentiments. As the Macy's continued to battle out their separation in 1916, she and a finger-spelling fellow socialist, Peter Fagan, made secret plans to marry in November. About the time she had met Fagan, in June 1916, thirty-six-year-old Helen gave an unusual and almost flippant interview to the *Chicago Tribune* on love and marriage. Her "unique opinions" were "pounded . . . out on her fingers and the face of her teacher." She refused to give the specifics of her romantic life but hinted that "a certain young man" was "attentive at this time." She described her ideal as a "handsome" man, necessary for "eugenic reasons," who "must be one who thinks straight." She said he did not have to be rich, for "I am paying my own passage through the world and am proud of it." The ardently political woman insisted that marriage was essential to civic health, since "there is no greater service to the state than a woman's gift of a child."[66]

How ideal Fagan was is unclear, but Keller's biographer, Dorothy Hermann, argues that probable physical contact between the two occurred that went beyond hand-holding. Once learning of the secretly made plans to marry, Helen's extended family and Anne vigorously squashed the relationship with forced midnight train trips out of town, an angry and gun-waving brother, and drama worthy of a bad novel. All felt adamantly that marriage and child-bearing were not options for a deaf-blind woman. With this pressure Helen apparently acquiesced to the belief. Peter Fagan disappeared from her life. Not only did her family and Anne hold eugenic fears about her possible reproduction and sexuality, but also many state laws prohibited women with disabilities from marriage and children.[67]

Helen found herself isolated in her mother's new community of Montgomery, Alabama, while everyone around her knew of the debated NAACP letter. She left little self-analysis of the period for historians. Presumably, she grieved the loss of Fagan. Perhaps her family, Anne Macy's departure, the color line of Alabama, and the way so many understood her disability angered her. "Parties, dresses, babies, weddings—and obesity are the topics of conversation," she complained to Anne, while Anne sought solace in Puerto Rico.[68]

Later in her life Keller subtly subverted the dismissal of Peter Fagan. Twice she publicly credited Alexander Graham Bell with encouraging her, during these years, to accept the possibility of marriage and children. In an article memorializing him after his death, she claimed that he had once come upon her when she was looking downcast. When she admitted that she was mourning the impossibility of love (in theory—not with anyone specific in mind), he had told her, "do not think that because you cannot see or hear, you are debarred from the supreme happiness of womanhood." Because she had lost her sight and hearing in a nonhereditary illness, marriage and children were a possibility in Bell's opinion. As a fifty-year-old woman, she claimed she had had Bell's support for marriage and childbearing. Publicly, however, she never argued against efforts to squelch her romantic life or against eugenic sentiments regarding marriage and childbearing for people with disabilities, generally. No evidence exists that the reported conversation took place other than from Keller herself. One wonders if the story was of her own making, a subtle attack on those who had earlier tried to restrict her own life, or a public effort to rewrite her own history by asserting that she *could* have married had she wanted. Or perhaps it was an expression of regret that she did not listen to Bell, instead yielding to the pressure of others.[69]

Life satisfied neither Keller nor Macy during the war and postwar period, as each strained for personal, economic, and professional stability. Seeking money, both agreed to a Hollywood production of Keller's life, *Deliverance*, in 1919. While they were in Hollywood, stage hands and actors struck, forcing Keller to make her political and class stance less theoretical. The media swarmed when she threatened not to appear at the premiere unless the strikers' cause advanced. Studios strongly hawked the film along with publicity photos of Keller, Macy, and Hollywood stars Mary Pickford, Douglas Fairbanks, and Charlie Chaplin. The opening of *Deliverance* was to be a major event. Fortunately, for the financial backers of the film, union and studio mediations began before the movie's premiere. That Keller influenced the strike outcome is unlikely.[70]

Deliverance symbolized Keller and Macy's floundering. Economic problems still persisted. Neither woman felt a strong sense of purpose. Editors only wanted to publish Keller's writings about herself, a subject on which she no longer cared to write. Structural impediments and the limiting expectations everyone had for a deaf-blind woman frustrated her political activism. Romance, marriage, and children appeared unlikely for either woman. Grasping for solutions, the two performed on the vaudeville circuit from 1920, when Keller was forty years old, until 1924. In the midst of this, in 1921, Helen's mother died.[71]

This was not what Keller had anticipated for herself as she had basked in the glow of a Radcliffe degree. During this period she knew that she did not like the world as it was but struggled to find a venue by which to seek alternatives.

Critics of all sorts disparaged Keller's entry into politics in the first decades of the century, just as critics had debated her capacities prior to and during her enrollment at Radcliffe. Editors and the reading public generally wanted nothing from her but uplifting commentaries on conquering disability. Political opponents questioned her capabilities and attacked her colleagues for misleading and manipulating her. According to detractors and sometimes according to well-intentioned supporters, her blindness and deafness rendered her politically disabled and thus incapable of independent and reasoned political opinions. They considered her unfit for a broad-ranging civic life. These ideas of *civic fitness*—historical and cultural definitions of who is fit for civic life and the relationship of those definitions to our bodies—shaped her public life.[72]

The press first blamed Anne and John Macy for filling Keller's head with leftist nonsense, calling them "enthusiastic Marxist propagandists." When her letter and donation to the NAACP became public knowledge, an Alabama newspaper attributed it to the couple's Yankee influence.[73] But the pair were soon forgotten, as Keller's political opponents repeatedly imputed her political beliefs to the influence on her of the larger radical movement, the effects of her disability, or both. For example, when it was rumored that Schenectady, New York's socialist city government would soon appoint her to the public welfare board (this never came to pass), critics wrote: "It would be difficult to imagine anything more pathetic than the present exploitation of poor Helen Keller by the Socialists of Schenectady." Another journalist wrote that her socialism was due to "the manifest limitations of her development." Her later friend Nella Braddy Henney characterized Keller as "in shock" and "outraged" when critics assumed that many of the ideas in *Out of the Dark* were "not hers."[74] Her critics could not conceive of her as capable of independent political thought and presumed that someone must have manipulated her.

Throughout the 1910s, Keller tried repeatedly to confront the politics of civic fitness head on: "I plead guilty," she said, "to the charge that I am deaf and blind," but she adamantly declared herself capable of understanding contemporary events: "I claim my right to discuss them."[75] "My blindness does not shut me out from a knowledge of what is happening about me." She read extensively in Braille (in several languages), was familiar with contemporary thinkers, and had magazines and newspapers from all over the world read to her. In fact, she insisted, "I have the advantage of a mind trained to think, and that is the difference between myself and most people, not my blindness and their sight." To those who would pity her, she rejoined, "I do not want their pity; I would not change places with one of them. I know what I am talking about." She rejected those who imagined her "in the hands of unscrupulous persons who lead me astray and persuade me to espouse unpopular causes and make me the mouthpiece of their propaganda." In a wonderful twist which emphasized her gender, her disability, and the ways she relied on different senses than her detractors, she argued that she had skills—skills unique to a woman with a disability—that they did not have: "Let them remember, though, that if I cannot see the fire at the end of their cigarettes, neither can they thread a needle in the dark." Keller claimed the right to political opinions and insisted that her opinions were as well reasoned, if not better, than those who thought of themselves as *normal* and *whole*.[76]

Just as she had had to explain how she perceived the world to justify her intellect as a young woman (her 1908 book *The World I Live In* is a prime example), she felt forced to justify how she literally perceived politics. Besides reading and conversation, she cited physical sensations. As an example, in 1913 she told of visiting sweatshops, factories, crowded slums, strike lines, and mining towns: "Of course I could not see the squalor; but if I could not see it, I could smell it. With my own hands I could feel pinched, dwarfed children tending their younger brothers and sisters, while their mothers tended machines in nearby factories."[77]

By her political expressions, Keller indicated that she assumed herself fit for participation in civic life, yet she did acknowledge external and internal limitations on that participation. But those limitations were not her deafness or blindness. In her political writings from approximately 1900 to the mid-1920s, the limitation she acknowledged was that of being female—the *gendered* body. When protesting the arrest and conviction of a defender of union activists, she discussed the tenuousness of her political participation by saying, "I have arrived at this conclusion with some hesitancy. For a mere woman, denied participation in government, must needs speak timidly of the mysterious mental processes of men."[78] Discussing her reluctance to speak about the conditions of poverty that contributed to blindness, she wrote:

> Moreover, the subject was one of which a young woman might be supposed to be ignorant, and upon which, certainly, she would not be expected to speak with authority. It is always painful to set one's self against tradition, especially against the conventions and prejudices that hedge about womanhood.[79]

Though Keller acknowledged that the barriers rooted in her gender caused her to hesitate in her civic expressions, she insisted that it should not be so. Just as paternity did not "incapacitate" the bodies of men for citizenship, she argued that the possibility of maternity should not render women's bodies unfit for citizenship.[80] She failed, however, to mention the citizenship of the disabled body.

The identity politics Keller tried to espouse was gender-based. Leaning toward a gender essentialism, she argued that women had unique knowledge, responsibilities, and skills that gave them political energy. This sense of obligation and mission was common among the first generations of female college students in the United States. In her effort to position herself as a political actor who centered her political identity in her gender, Keller joined a wide array of early twentieth-century female activists. Her declaration that "woman's place is still in the household. But the household is more spacious than in times gone by," echoed the sentiments of many other women interested in the tasks of politicized domesticity. In this period many women, from a wide political spectrum, used gender-based arguments to justify and explain their political sensibilities and to claim civic fitness.[81]

Perhaps Keller embraced a gender-based political identity strategically, to claim civic fitness by acknowledging the metaphorical disability of gender rather than the physical impairments of blindness or deafness, because she thought this would least limit her. By claiming a *gendered* body, she may have sought to seize control of the way she defined herself and others defined her. Again, however, in the eyes and laws of the society in which she lived she was not simply female, for she embodied both a gender and a disability status.

Despite her vigorous claims of civic fitness, Keller remained fairly isolated in this period from possible political and ideological allies, most markedly the strong world of female reform and activism. During her years at Radcliffe and due to her interest in radicalism and reform, she met many leading female activists and knew of many others. What differentiated her was her relative lack of involvement in the networks of club women, settlement house workers, peace advocates, union organizers, social scientists, and legislative campaigners. She met political women, corresponded with them, and occasionally spoke in public forums, but remained on the sidelines of the rich emotional and organized public work of radical and reformist women. Activist women who encountered her tended to use the extravagant language employed by Emma Goldman, who praised her for having "overcome the most appalling physical disability." Keller filled a similar symbolic role for the radical political movement of the early twentieth century as she did later for the American Foundation for the Blind. Her personal appeal could solicit funds, her presence could draw an audience, her public image could incite renewed passion for the cause, and her words could guarantee media attention. For Goldman, as for many others, Keller's disability made her an inspirational novelty, not a comrade.[82]

2

The Call of
the Sightless

1924–1937

Before I left Radcliffe I had heard the call of the sightless.
—Helen Keller, 1929

Helen Keller entered the 1920s seeking a meaningful public life and adequate financial support for personal stability. The newly created American Foundation for the Blind (AFB) supplied both, becoming the center of her and Anne Macy's lives. Founded in 1921, the AFB united a coalition of the American Association for the Instruction of the Blind and the American Association of Workers for the Blind. Businessman and primary donor M.C. ("Major") Migel, the organization's first president, figured prominently in Keller's life. At the organization's founding, longtime worker for blind people, Charles Campbell, told Migel that the wealthy nearly threw money at her feet. Migel knew the AFB needed Helen and Anne if it was to have national impact.[1]

Keller had found it impossible to have the political and publishing life she desired. Macy's earning potential was very limited and her health in flux. Their financial precariousness, compounded by Anne's ill health, seemingly put them in a weak negotiating position with the AFB. On the other hand, the pair wielded a unique celebrity that gave them immense bargaining power. Macy led talks with the AFB. As biographer Joseph Lash describes it, any teamster negotiator would have been proud. Over the fall of 1924, she arranged a $2,000 monthly salary and a detailed plan to raise a two-million-dollar endowment. She extracted a $1,000 gift from Migel to cover their current bills. Migel and others in the AFB rejoiced over Keller's increasing distance from radical politics, but her endorsement of Senator Robert La Follette for president that fall alarmed them. Lash concluded that Keller softened her politics at the request of the foundation.[2]

The AFB's decision to hire the pair paid off for the foundation. News of the first fund-raising meeting—which raised $21,000—bore the headline "PURSES FLY OPEN TO HELEN KELLER." President Calvin Coolidge agreed to serve as honorary chairman of the AFB. By 1924, it provided the bulk of their income and cemented Keller's public identification with the cause of blindness. She and Macy had already lectured to over 250,000 people at 249 meetings in 123 cities. It became the dominant organization pertaining to blindness in the United States. She remained affiliated with the AFB for the rest of her life, as blindness became her primary public focus.[3]

Keller's growing political cautiousness had many causes. The antiradicalism and conservatism of the period played a major role. The conservative businessmen who largely led and funded the AFB did not take kindly to her political views and let her know it. Others who had expressed sentiments similar to hers were deported, arrested, or pressured into silence. Among them was John Macy's good friend Arturo Giovannitti, who had frequently corresponded with Keller and visited their home. In the face of organized antifeminism and dissension within the progressive female community, many women limited their political activities. Keller may have felt these same pressures. She may also have become more circumspect politically because of periodic crises in Anne Macy's health throughout the late 1910s and 1920s. Anne's inability to join her on speaking tours restricted Helen's activities. She worried greatly about her good friend, who had never approved of her political radicalism.[4]

Substantial evidence indicates that Keller also altered her political behavior in response to stereotyped and limiting perceptions of disability. In 1924, Wisconsin Senator Robert La Follette received the presidential nomination of the Farmer-Labor ticket. A month later, Keller publicly released a letter to him, apologizing for her tardiness, but explaining that she had hesitated to write. She feared what newspapers opposed to him would say about his political movement and its manipulation of her if she endorsed him publicly:

> It would be difficult to imagine anything more fatuous and stupid than the attitude of the press toward anything I say on public affairs. So long as I confine my activities to social service and the blind, they compliment me extravagantly, calling me "archpriestess of the sightless," "wonder woman" and "a modern miracle." But when it comes to a discussion of poverty, and I maintain that it is the result of wrong economics . . . that is a different matter! . . . I do not mind having my ideas attacked and my aims opposed and ridiculed, but it is not fair fighting or good argument to find that "Helen Keller's mistakes spring out of the limitations of her development."

The quandary she found herself in, she wrote, "explains my silence on subjects which are of vital interest to me."[5] Despite this, she figured publicly in the La Follette campaign. Indeed, she served as "Colonel" of the New York City "Fighting Bobs" (La Follette's campaign team)—a task that included numerous public appearances. She corresponded with both Robert and his wife Belle La Follette throughout the fall and spoke at La Follette events at least three times. After the La Follette campaign, however, her public activism on a wide range of issues diminished almost entirely. The frustration she felt was very real. Her detractors and political opponents succeeded in doing what her blindness and deafness had not. They robbed her of her political voice, denying her the full expression of citizenship.

Keller did not buy into the contention that her disability disqualified her from civic fitness. Nor did she acquiesce simply in order to protect her livelihood. The numerous obstacles caused by interpretations of her disability made the political participation she desired increasingly difficult for many private and public reasons. The antiradicalism of the 1920s accompanied growing national concern about the *body* of the U.S. citizenry. The growing popularity of eugenic sentiments reflected the sharpened concern about the physical "fitness" of American citizens. Medical and educational experts increasingly viewed people with disabilities as within the realm of their expertise and sought to "cure" or to "shelter" them in medical arenas. Tightened immigration restrictions made it increasingly difficult for a person with a disability to become a legal citizen. This context, coupled with her political views, limited the effectiveness of Keller's claims to civic fitness.[6]

As a result, by the mid-1920s, as Keller reached her mid-forties, she narrowed her public political activities to focus almost exclusively on the AFB. In some ways this concentration served her well. On behalf of the AFB she traveled, raised funds, lobbied political leaders, as well as state and national legislatures, and became an international star. She made a comfortable living, visited over thirty foreign countries, met numerous international figures, and was considered by the State Department one of the most effective public representatives of the United States overseas. In Eleanor Roosevelt's words, she was "a goodwill ambassador of the U.S."[7] The AFB relied extensively on her for fund-raising and political lobbying in the 1920s, 1930s, and 1940s, confident that her signature at the bottom of a fund-raising letter, a personal letter from her, or a personal appearance, could raise large sums of money or sway a legislature.[8]

The political identity Keller somewhat reluctantly embraced in public after the mid-1920s was that of a *blind person* whose civic interests and knowledge revolved around *blindness*. Though she commented several times in her life that she felt "the impediment of deafness far more keenly than that of blindness," her personal history made ties with deaf people and the Deaf community difficult. Her experience had taught her that public expression of a broad-ranging civic fitness was difficult, and that it was further narrowed by antiradicalism and by public expectations of someone with her disability. This was, quite literally, a politics of the body. She seems to have escaped one stereotype only to move to another: from the politically manipulated and publicly pitied, deaf and blind young virgin to the politically safe, but glorified, superblind saintly spinster. Both stereotypes emphasized her *difference*, separating her from a normal social network.[9]

This persona, however, was an incredibly effective fund-raiser. In 1928, the AFB launched the Helen Keller Endowment Fund, seeking to provide a $2 million financial base for the seven-year-old organization.[10] Keller's fame and the AFB's legitimacy were such that the Endowment attracted others of influence. For example, alongside an editorial, the *New York Times* published a lengthy letter from her, explaining the function and tasks of the AFB, mentioning the publication of her new book *Midstream*, and encouraging readers to give to the Endowment Fund. The editorial encouraged all to read her letter, to give their funds, and thanked her for her work: "We are grateful to Miss Keller for making us see what would remain invisible except to the clear vision of an understanding mind and heart." It was a fund-raiser's fantasy come true.[11]

As Keller and AFB President M. C. Migel grew in experience, they developed a system. Someone from the AFB went to a site to prepare arrangements. Out of a tea came a committee and a date for Keller to visit. She arrived for a large meeting and a smaller tea with potential major donors. In receiving lines she insisted on knowing everyone's name. A local representative introduced guests to Polly Thompson, the newest addition to the Keller household, or Anne when her health allowed it. Helen then either spoke or finger-spelled to the guest. The local organization sponsoring the visit and the AFB split any contributions. AFB activist and future president Robert Barnett described her persuasive powers as immense: "I never got one negative answer to an appeal from her. If she walked into a room, it was like an angel."[12]

While Keller primarily focused on the AFB and its subsidiaries, she devoted limited fund-raising time to other organizations. Throughout the 1930s and 1940s, she attended events, making financial appeals, for the Palestinian Lighthouse. Largely funded by U.S. Jewish women, this organization provided educational and rehabilitative assistance for blind people in what was to become Israel.[13] She also supported the efforts of the Lions, a philanthropic organization of U.S. men that devoted time and funds to assisting blind people internationally. She called the Lions her "knights of the blind."[14]

Not only could Keller raise money, but on behalf of the AFB she also was an unparalleled lobbyist. As Migel noted, "Only a heart of stone could fail to respond to an appeal from Helen Keller." Legislators were "spellbound," wept, and reportedly "adjourned temporarily to greet her."[15] In the 1930s and 1940s, she either visited or wrote targeted letters to at least eighteen weepy state legislatures, most often encouraging funding for or creation of state commissions for the blind.[16] Other causes included funding for educational institutions for blind people, bills to allow blind persons to travel with a guide on public transportation for one fare, and funds for Braille books. Sometimes the AFB initiated the visits, sometimes local organizations wrote to the AFB seeking her assistance, sometimes local organizations wrote her directly. In almost every case, the AFB was eventually involved. The numerous letters of thanks she received testify to her effectiveness.[17] She also lobbied, occasionally in person but most frequently via telegram or letter, the U.S. Congress and U.S. presidents.

AFB officials could be quite specific in their requests to Keller. For example, in 1933, Migel urged that she ask Franklin Roosevelt to support a bill allowing blind people to run newsstands in federal office buildings. In 1934, while she was in Scotland on holiday, Migel asked her to cable the New Jersey governor on behalf of legislation allowing blind persons to travel with a guide on public transportation for one fare. He also suggested that she give the governor permission to publicize the cable. Before she and AFB Executive Director Bob Irwin visited the U.S. House Committee, Irwin briefed her on who they were going to visit and likely successful arguments.[18]

Keller and the AFB enthusiastically supported the Social Security Act. When it first passed in 1935, as the Wagner Economic Security Act, she allowed her name to be put on the amendment proposed by Senator Robert Wagner (NY, Democrat) to expand vocational training for blind people. Lobbying on behalf of the measure, she emphasized the amendment's economic as well as human benefits.[19] In 1944, she urged expansion of the Social Security Act to support "the particular needs of the poorer blind." Her testimony before the House Labor Committee highlighted the circumstances of "the colored blind" and "the deaf-blind." These were, she said, "the hardest pressed and least cared-for" among her "blind fellows."[20]

Keller apparently complied with the vast majority of these requests, but sometimes she disagreed and refused. For example, when Robert Barnett asked her in 1943 to write to the Senate Finance Committee chair in support of a clause in the tax bill, allowing blind persons to take a flat deduction of $500 to offset expenses incurred because of blindness, she said no. The legislation was not "vitally important," she declared. She noted that she and Barnett were "fairly comfortable," but that the majority of blind people had so little income that they paid no income tax. She sought to "promote the well-being of those caught in the double tragedy of being poor and blind." As a result, instead of a tax deduction, she supported federal insurance against blindness. Barnett's letter of reply acknowledged her arguments and made a half-hearted effort to persuade her otherwise, but it seems clear he did not expect to change her mind.[21]

The immense success of Keller as a fund-raiser and lobbyist reveals the strength and power she held as a public figure. In that role she was unparalleled. Her fame perhaps tells us more about U.S. culture than about her. She was the famous deaf-blind woman—famous for her disability, famous for her cheerful countenance, famous for the innocence presumably ensured her by the lack of sight and hearing, famous for her ability to continue *despite*. One highly publicized day of crass and crabby behavior, or as the AFB feared—un-American politics, would have scratched this pristine public image. She succeeded as a fund-raiser and lobbyist because she reminded others of what they had and did not want to think about losing, namely, sight and hearing. She then artfully asked for assistance—but only for others—while never inducing guilt. The giving, adoring, and revering public responded because she literally embodied an understanding of disability with which it felt comfortable.

Throughout the 1920s, Keller's public life remained integrally tied to the AFB. She served as its major fund-raiser and slowly began to move into political lobbying, in which she would engage more fully in the 1930s and early 1940s. Privately, she tried to write on topics other than her childhood self, while struggling with Anne Macy's depression at her own deteriorating eyesight.

In 1927, Nella Braddy Henney joined Keller's entourage. The manuscript that was to become *Midstream*, a continuation of her 1903 autobiography, was going nowhere. Anne was unable to assist and the hostile separation of Anne and John Macy made his editorial assistance unfeasible. Ken McCormick, her editor at the publishing company Doubleday, sent Henney, a literary agent and assistant editor, to facilitate the writing of the book. Keller notified the AFB that she was taking a leave from work. Her relationship with Henney was at first bumpy. Henney originally didn't know finger-spelling. Helen and John Macy had developed an editing process that worked for them. The method she and Henney first adopted prompted her to insist on changes. The emerging text, she complained to Henney, "is more yours than mine." As a result, the two adopted a new method, meaning that Henney spent ten to seventeen hours a day with Helen during her visits to the Keller household in Forest Hills, New York.[22]

Henney became an integral part of the Keller household, and the woman fourteen years younger than Helen remained an intimate friend until a bitter break-up in 1960. She venerated Anne Sullivan Macy, considering her and her teaching methods brilliant. Later, she would publish an uncritical biography exalting Anne, *Anne Sullivan Macy: The Story Behind Helen Keller* (1933). The Georgia native married Keith Henney, also a Doubleday editor, and never had children. Helen became her purpose. As Keller biographer Dorothy Herrmann puts it, Henney "regarded herself as Teacher's [Anne's] heir apparent," undertaking the responsibility of "educating" Helen about the larger world after Anne's death and monitoring Helen's behavior.[23]

The book first published by the pair was not the anticipated autobiography but *My Religion* (1927). Apparently, neither Nella nor Anne warmly supported the effort, but Helen insisted and Doubleday cooperated. To a Swedenborgian leader, she wrote, "it would be such a joy to me if I might be the instrument of bringing Swedenborg to a world that is spiritually deaf and blind." *My Religion* is designed to explain and draw others to the

Swedenborgian faith tradition. It introduces the reader to Emanuel Swedenborg, attempts to explain the basic tenets of his teachings, and describes her conversion. *My Religion*'s rambling and confusing nature perhaps reflects the toil and difficulty required for the trio to develop an intellectual and practical editing process that worked. It was not a widely popular book, but Helen treasured the opportunity to explain her faith. Concluding the book, she wrote, "I cannot imagine myself without religion. . . . To one who is deaf and blind, the spiritual world offers no difficulty."[24] Such a theology established her as a legitimate judge of and participant in the larger world.

The continued work on *Midstream* agonized the household. Neither Helen nor Anne completely trusted Nella yet, and Anne insisted on reviewing material before letting Nella see it. Helen typed drafts on the manual typewriter that accompanied her virtually everywhere. Nella read these drafts to Anne, whose eyesight remained weak. Nella and Anne then literally cut and pasted editorial changes, Nella read them to Anne while Anne finger-spelled the drafts to Helen, and the process would start again. Anne insisted that some material on herself be excluded, hoping not only to write her own book but also to keep some material from becoming public. Helen struggled with what to say about her politics and her romance with Peter Fagan.[25]

Finally, in 1929, Doubleday published *Midstream*. The book received some attention, but the reading public cared less about her adult life than her dramatic childhood acquisition of language. Helen missed John Macy's editorial advice and personal friendship. In *Midstream*, she wrote fondly of John, "if this book is not what it should be, it is because I feel lonely and bewildered without his supporting hand." She sent him a copy of the book, one wonders if Anne knew, and he responded with praise. She wrote him again with thanks: "always you were in my mind, and how I longed for your reassuring approval!"[26]

The books took energy, but Anne's eyesight dominated the concerns of the household in the late 1920s. She was the famous Teacher of deaf-blind Helen Keller, but she also was visually impaired. She had enrolled at

Perkins School for the Blind because she was blind. Surgeries while she was a student there, and repeated medical treatments then and later, improved her eyesight, but throughout her life it remained highly variable. In 1929, she had one eye removed and a cataract was growing over the other. Helen wrote that between 1927 and 1930, "the sorrow that oppressed me was the knowledge of her coming total blindness."[27]

As an educator and friend to Helen, Anne believed firmly that blindness should be no deterrent. Helen proudly asserted that Anne "believed in the blind not as a class apart but as human beings endowed with rights." She insisted that Anne "never allowed anyone to pity me to adopt the over protectiveness that can render blindness such a tragedy. She did not allow people to praise anything I did unless I did it well, and resented it with spirit if anyone addressed himself to her instead of to me as they would to a normal child."[28]

In contradiction to this, however, Anne responded to her own deteriorating eyesight with depression and isolation. Increasingly, she was physically incapable of performing the tasks she had undertaken for Helen, and increasingly, she was temperamentally unable to handle the changes in her own life. The pair depended more and more on Polly Thomson.

Anne's response to her deteriorating eyesight reveals an unsettling understanding of her own disability, and thus of Helen's and of disability, in general, as a degrading tragedy reflective of personal and physical failure. Anne considered her own blindness to be deeply shameful. As Helen later wrote:

She was one of those sensitive spirits that feel ashamed by blindness. It humiliates them like a stupid blunder or a deformed limb. They do not count on the compassionate understanding of others, and they shrink from the comments of those who watch their struggle against misfortune. Blindness is a blow to their freedom and dignity, especially when they have always been active and industrious. . . . She feared to become wholly a burden and troublesome to those who cared for her.[29]

Portrait of Helen Keller, Anne Sullivan, and Polly Thomson, 1932. Sullivan's Scottish terrier, probably Darky, and Keller's Great Dane, probably Helga, are included. *Courtesy of the American Foundation for the Blind. Used with permission of the American Foundation for the Blind, Helen Keller Archives.*

Anne desperately hid her disability from public knowledge and retreated into seclusion. Nella Braddy Henney cooperated when she published her 1933 biography of the famed teacher and said little of Anne's lifelong disability. The efforts of both women have contributed to the dominant historical perception of Anne as sighted or only slightly visually impaired. Perhaps Anne assumed it would detract from her reputation as a stellar and innovative teacher. Whatever she thought, the lessons she had stridently taught to Helen she was unable to apply to herself. One wonders if Helen ever grew frustrated or angry or if Helen questioned what Anne had taught her.

In the early 1930s, intense personal concerns about Anne's health, her own efforts to write, and growing fund-raising and lobbying responsibilities for the AFB continued to consume Helen's life. In 1932, she wrote to Nella in frustration, "How I wish I might be invisible for five months! The truth is, I find that I'm beginning to hate compliments, messages, tributes and photographs. The effort to take them graciously strains my 'love ye one another' principle to the breaking-point. The grateful smile I wear on all occasions is becoming 'fixed' on my face, and won't come off when I go to bed." Despite this, she sought continued involvement and interests in a political life. Clearly it interested her, and perhaps it was a distraction from other concerns. She repeatedly resisted conforming to the political desires of AFB leaders. In 1932, she told the *New York Times* that she was "still a Socialist" but mitigated her statement somewhat by reassuring readers that she was too busy with the AFB to vote: "I am not bothering with politics."[30]

Keller, however, watched growing war tensions in Europe closely. In the 1930s, her limited public discussions of peace tended to focus on the world-transformative possibilities of women and female maternalism. By raising children to value harmony, she argued, women could "throw our weight in the scale on the side of peace." In a sermon reported in the *New York Times*, her point was sharper as she warned that neither the League of Nations, nor the world disarmament conference in Geneva, nor tariffs and moratoriums would bring peace. Because the "acquisitive motives" of rulers were the primary cause of war, only increased knowledge and "spiritual vision" on the part of citizens could bring peace.[31]

Keller followed German politics with great trepidation. She knew of and feared Hitler earlier than most Americans. When Nazi students burned books exemplifying "the un-German spirit" in 1933—and included hers in the bonfire—she responded quickly with a letter released through the Associated Press, stating emphatically that ideas could not be destroyed.[32] Returning to the United States after nearly fourteen months in Scotland in 1934, she "sharply rebuked" Hitler and Mussolini for their militarism and ideologies of hate, saying that she continually followed the news until "my fingers refuse to go on and I shudder and quit."[33] She feared what the rise of Hitler would mean for Jews and people with disabilities. Her Associated Press statement of 1933 included the warning to Nazi students that "do not imagine your barbarities to the Jews are unknown here. God sleepeth not, and He will visit His judgment upon you."[34]

Keller's lengthy visits to Europe contributed to her awareness of European tensions. Between 1930 and 1935 she, Anne, and Polly traveled three times to Scotland for lengthy visits. Both Anne and Helen found refuge in the home of Polly's brother Robert, a minister in the Church of Scotland, and his family. The trips provided privacy, solace, and a slower pace. They also created and reinforced Helen's pattern of depending on travel as escape, refuge, and perhaps distraction.

On the first of these trips, the trio almost obsessively corresponded with their friend Amelia Bond, Migel's secretary, about John Macy's latest book *About Women* (1930). Unfortunately, their comments haven't survived, but Helen, Anne, and Polly apparently agreed with a fairly negative *New York Times* review.[35] The book insists that it "is not an attack on women" but clearly criticized contemporary women for being too forthright and dismissed women's claims to greater public and personal involvement. Anne's estranged husband criticized "interfering women who try to run the whole show and reform the male actors" and warned of "a lack of logic in the processes of the feminine mind" (but fondly wrote that "that defect . . . may be part of their charm"). In 1932, John Macy died and left Anne a widow, the widow of a man she had not seen but had refused to divorce for almost twenty years. She paid for his funeral.[36]

Anne's overall health also continued to deteriorate. In 1932, Migel promised Anne that the AFB would make sure Helen was cared for and legal arrangements were made for a separate committee of three trustees to administer Helen's finances. With Migel and Franklin Roosevelt's help, Polly secured legal immigration and eventually citizenship status. Nella's 1933 biography of Anne appeared with the implicit urgency of her ill health. In April 1935, doctors operated on her other eye, but it only caused her to rapidly lose most of her remaining sight.[37]

Anne Sullivan Macy's death on October 20, 1936, surprised no one. She was seventy years old. The book she had always said she would write remained unwritten. She left all documents relating to Helen to Nella, with the arrangement that Nella would assist Helen with any further literary works. AFB officials and friends celebrated her life with a large funeral at the National Cathedral. The woman who spent her childhood as an orphan in the infamous Tewksbury Almshouse had traveled far.

Almost immediately after Anne's funeral, Helen and Polly made plans to return to Scotland and the sanctuary of Polly's brother's home. Aboard the ship *Deutschland* only two weeks after Anne's death, Helen wrote, "This is the first voyage Polly and I have had without Teacher, who was the life and the center of our journeyings by land and sea. . . . The anguish which makes me feel cut in two prevents me from writing another word about these life-wrecking changes." The loss of such a vital partner made her "deaf-blind a second time." In *My Religion* (1927), she had written that she "believe[d] that in heaven friendships may endure, as indeed they do on earth, by changing as well as by their steadfastness." Swedenborg taught her that the wall between the material world and the spiritual world was permeable. In her pain she tried to hold steadfast to the spirit of Anne. In her 1956 book *Teacher*, she wrote, "Now and here I am in the spiritual world where my life will continue to eternity when I awake from this earth-dream; therefore I have never felt that Teacher and I were really apart."[38]

The more than two months in "the manse," as Helen called the Scottish parsonage, soothed her. She ate good food, thrilled to the slow and earnest finger-spelling of Polly's nephews, followed European and U.S. politics

Portrait of Keller near Orkney Islands, 1932. *Courtesy of the American Foundation for the Blind. Used with permission of the American Foundation for the Blind, Helen Keller Archives.*

closely, while the entire household obsessed about King Edward's abdication. At some points she despaired, writing once that "I have experienced a sense of dying daily. Every hour I long for the thousand bright signals from her vital, beautiful hand." At others she felt hope: "This morning I awoke positively sure I had seen Teacher, and I have been happier all day."[39]

During Anne's last months in 1936, Helen had received a visit from Takeo Iwahashi. Iwahashi was an English-speaking Christian, the director of the Osaka Lighthouse (the primary school for blind people in Japan), and Japanese translator of *The Story of My Life*. He thrilled her by urging that she visit Japan. According to Keller, when Anne heard of it, she insisted that Helen "promise me that after I am gone you and Polly will be light-bringers to the handicapped of Japan." The AFB's M. C. Migel encouraged the trip.[40] In December, Iwahashi contacted her at the manse, urging her to visit Japan in the spring. Helen characterized it as "the call of destiny." She referred to the trip with energy: "There are hard problems to be solved before Polly and I can enter upon a work of such scope and international significance, but we are resolved to accomplish it somehow."[41]

Returning to the home she had shared with Anne scared her. From London she wrote, "I have only begun to climb my Calvary of love. . . . Too well I know how often Teacher will seem to die again as I go from room to room, object to object, and find her not." As she sailed into New York harbor, grief overpowered her: "this finality about our earthly separation seemed more than I could bear." People often spoke to her of blindness and deafness as "monstrous afflictions," but she reflected that "there is no test so pitiless and searching as this sorrow."[42]

Once home in early February 1937, she busied herself with necessary preparations for her April 1 departure from San Francisco for Japan. Nothing, however, was right. In late February, she complained of others trying to manage her life: "A GUST of irritability is blowing through me just now because there has been a recurrence of a tendency in some people to try to run my affairs. . . . There are still those who appear to think it is incumbent upon them to alter my life course according to their own ideas!" On March

3, her "soul birthday," as she called the anniversary of Anne's arrival in her life, her good friend and the household's caretaker, Herbert Haas, entered the hospital gravely ill. "From the moment I wake in the morning until I lie down at night," she wrote, "there is an ache at my heart which never stops."[43]

Keller's and Henney's memoirs frame Keller's interest in Japan as the result of the 1936 death-bed promise exacted by Anne, never as a personal desire to travel or to involve herself in international politics. The 1937 trip certainly met the profound personal needs of Helen, grief-stricken after the death of Anne, and unsure of the rest of her life. Travel also, however, kept her in the public realm and kept the public closely within her realm. She had, in the terms of her biographer Joseph Lash, an "almost compulsive need to travel. . . . Behind it was her ever-lurking fear that it was easy for the world to overlook the deaf-blind Helen Keller."[44]

The final departure seemed a relief and offered Keller the chance to look forward. Crossing the Nevada desert by train, she recalled the deaths of both Anne and her mother, "As I contemplate the immeasurable changes in my life since the death-curtain fell between them and me, this country, not Japan, seems the foreign land." Aboard the *Asama-Maru*, sailing under the Golden Gate Bridge, she expressed excitement and purpose for the first time in several years.

> I exulted in the thought of new horizons opening before my mind. Perhaps that was the beginning of my release from the torturing sense that a world had been burnt out with Teacher's passing. Certainly she seemed nearer than she had since she last kissed me. My purpose was revitalized, as if she had spoken from her celestial home encouraging me to go forth into the darknesses and the silences yet untouched by hope.

She and Polly Thompson left, carrying messages of goodwill from President Roosevelt to the people of Japan, hopes to meet "the progressive women" of Japan, and with metaphorical expressions of Keller's usual style: "What could be more fitting than for the land of the rising sun to be the center of a new hope, so that light shall shine on those who sit in the great darkness?"[45]

The two weeks on ship gave Keller additional opportunity to look forward. Her journal of the trip focuses on speech preparations and *Gone With the Wind*. The eighteen-volume Braille version of *Gone With the Wind* caused her to reflect on her Alabama childhood and her present life. She was fifty-seven years old and looked back with both nostalgia and a greater sense of racial and class awareness. When not mentally in Alabama, she prepared speeches without Anne's assistance for the first time. She despaired of the difficulties of oral speech. She feared that the blind people of Japan would pay the cost of her failure. "After breakfast I wrote and rewrote the speeches until I felt mentally black and blue. They must be as short as possible if I am not to overtax my listeners' patience with my halting delivery, and I am anxious to put over as many worth-while ideas as I can in my pleas for the Japanese blind."[46]

Helen's published memoir of this period ends on April 14, 1937, Anne's birthday. She had been dead almost six months. As Helen prepared to debark from the *Asama-Maru*, Anne's absence still pained her: "When I awoke this morning, I started to find Teacher and tell her somehow my joy that the world had been blessed in her birth. Then I remembered and was transfixed with pain. There was no language for my yearning to see her." At the same time, and in accord with the teachings of Swedenborg, Helen insisted that Anne was with them, for "strength flows into us for tasks to which we never dreamed we would be equal." The imminent arrival in Japan and the opportunities of the trip thrilled her. She took from Anne's death a renewed and more deeply passionate sense of purpose. From hence forward, she would focus on "the call of the sightless" internationally.

> Having come thus far, she will reinforce my labours with an inner power given only to those who have loved deeply and believed unwaveringly. . . . And as I stood on deck this morning in the mist of dawn, looking westward to the land where a Great Adventure awaits me, I thought I could feel her by my side.[47]

3

Manna in
My Desert Places

1937–1948

> After the intellectual hunger I often have felt since
> Teacher's going it is a priceless blessing to have such
> friends pour manna into my desert places.
> —Helen Keller, 1943

Keller's 1937 trip to Japan constituted almost pure pleasure. In Japan, where people had known of her since at least 1897, she drew huge crowds while visiting thirty-nine cities and giving ninety-seven lectures. Her friend Takeo Iwahashi served as translator. Buddhists at the ancient city of Nara honored her and Polly Thomson by allowing them to become the first women to touch the city's famed bronze Buddha. In a further rare privilege, the emperor and empress received her in a formal reception. According to one Japanese newspaper, "No foreign visitor had ever been accorded such an enthusiastic reception, not a prince, or president, Kaiser or king."[1]

In Japan, Helen felt her public presence to be effective. To a friend, she wrote, "we have succeeded in convincing the people that their handicapped can, if given a chance, become useful and reasonably happy human beings." Leaders of education for blind children planned to expand the Osaka Lighthouse for the Blind and build another in Tokyo. Her visit prompted national calls for greater governmental attention to "the welfare of the blind, deaf and dumb." A leader of the [Japanese] National Association for the Blind wrote to Migel upon her return, "Dr. Helen Keller's visit to Japan has already exerted more influence than any other goodwill mission on American-Japanese relations. Furthermore, her visit is giving all the people of our nation a new recognition of the blind and other physically handicapped groups." For Helen, who had constantly questioned the effectiveness and worth of her public work in the United States, Japan was a heady experience.[2]

Japan also provided an entirely new sensory experience. To her friend John Finley, she wrote:

> Never have I had so many ecstasies crowded into my touch—the arrangement of garden and shrubbery that perpetually changes like magic, the pines and other trees trimmed through centuries to the strangest shapes, the surprises of originality I discover even in small objects—the cups out of which I drink green tea, the fruit dishes, vases and screens. Vibrations, too, flow about me in surprising abundance. Sleeping on the tatami in Japanese hotels I have felt through the matting a myriad of soft little echoes from sliding door and window, the maids passing back and forth like a zephyr, the rustle of kimonos and the hum of voices and even the noises in the street outside. Truly Nippon has a glory for those who cannot see and a voice for those who cannot hear.

She sought, she told Finley, a "fitting return" for the joy of her visit. That return, she decided, was to "do my best to strengthen the bonds of amity between Nippon and the United States." She would be so thankful if Finley, a Westport neighbor and editor at the *New York Times*, would write "one of your precious paragraphs of good-will towards other countries."[3]

The U.S. federal government also realized the import of her visit. In 1937, war loomed between Japan and other parts of Asia, particularly China. The United States had a wary relationship with the potentially imperialistic country. In his public speech at Helen's departure, U.S. Ambassador Joseph C. Grew called her, in what was presumably intended as a compliment, "a second Admiral Perry": "Never before has an American created so great an atmosphere of friendship in Japan. . . . She is a second Admiral Perry, but whereas he opened the door with fear and suspicion, she has done it with love and affection." In Grew's private report to the secretary of state on her visit, which was forwarded to Roosevelt, he wrote, "The extent to which the achievements of Miss Keller, a woman of no official standing, appeal to the Japanese nation has been amply evidenced by the warm reception, largely official, which has been given her."[4]

Before Keller left Asia in late summer 1937, she toured Korea and Manchuria. Fearing war, AFB president Migel had attempted to stop her, but she sought travel for continued comfort. Anne's death still continued to weigh on her. Travel, she wrote to Migel, "is the only weapon against the most desolating and life-wrecking sorrow I have ever endured." Japan, however, invaded China. During her last month, she traveled in darkened trains and spoke in darkened auditoriums as a precaution against air raids. As she headed to Korea, she wrote to her friend and *New York Times* editor John Finley that the

> grim specter of war is stalking almost on our very tracks. Since hostilities recommenced between China and Nippon a week ago we have been traveling with soldiers. . . . Wherever we go we hear crowds shouting "Banzai! Banzai!" as the troops march northward. . . . It is impossible to guess what may happen the next moment. As we go to Mukden and Dairen we shall get closer to the Great Horror. My heart bleeds for the men who may be blinded, deafened and maimed on both sides. I can only hope war may be averted.

In August, the AFB announced that the trip to China was cancelled.[5]

Keller felt both relief and sorrow to leave Asia. She was "relieved to escape the horrible war atmosphere." As she explained to Finley, "I do not know whom I feel more sorry for—the long-enduring, shamefully insulted Chinese dying by the thousands for freedom they are beginning to understand, or the Japanese millions staggering under the heaviest taxation in their history."[6] She regretted leaving Takeo Iwahashi and his wife Keo. They had become dear friends and she was leaving them in what would likely become a war zone. She lamented leaving Asia without visiting

China but recognized what war meant and felt her visit to be fruitful. She may have felt her deathbed promise to Anne partially unfinished.

While abbreviated, Helen's 1937 trip to Japan was pivotal. She held deep affection for Takeo and Keo Iwahashi and the country. Aching from Anne's death, bored and unconvinced that her present work for the AFB accomplished much, she sought a new direction for her personal and professional energies. Japan centered her global travel, her global vision, and hopes for global harmony. Most important, the trip to Japan demonstrated to her, the AFB, and the federal government that she had international impact no one else could duplicate. Though it took several years to accomplish, she would build on this realization.

Once home, life bored her. In 1938, apparently evaluating her place in the world, she reflected on her work for blind people. Without conscious irony that her primary identification was with blindness and not deafness, she wrote, "Lack of hearing has always been a heavier handicap to me than blindness." Yet, she spoke of her decision to work for the AFB. She lamented "the impossibility of working for both the blind and the deaf, as I have often longed to do. . . . Reluctantly, therefore, I have confined my activities almost exclusively to the dwellers in the Dark Land."[7]

That same year, the nationally publicized case of five-week-old Helaine Colan offered Keller another public opportunity to discuss the implications of disability. These public pronouncements differed dramatically from those she had made in the 1915 Haiselden-Bolinger case. Colan needed both eyes removed if she were to live because of a rare disease that was attacking her eyes and would move to her brain. Her parents, it was reported across the nation, "were near collapse tonight from the terrific responsibility of their decision." They, ten doctors, and two rabbis sought to decide whether to choose blindness or death for the young girl.[8] Keller sent a wire and then a lengthy publicly released letter to the parents. "Blindness," she said, "is not the greatest evil. It is only a physical handicap which Helaine's mind can overcome. That is life."[9] Explaining her own feelings about the value of intellect, she claimed Helaine had the possibility of "a life which may be glorified with knowledge, vision more precious than sight." Like Jane Addams almost twenty years earlier, she argued that "the annals of progress show undeniably that much of humanity's finest work has been wrought by persons with a severe handicap." She closed her appeal with a claim that "all the handicapped" had a unique understanding of justice that Helaine could gain: "that she may be spared to help open the eyes of ignorance, soften insensibility in those who have eyes and see not." Rather than echoing earlier eugenic sentiments, she echoed her earlier arguments that the truly disabled were those who had "eyes of ignorance."[10]

Several months later, President Franklin Roosevelt offered Keller an important opportunity to confront ignorance about disability. In July, he invited her to serve on the Committee on Purchase of Products Made by the Blind. She and both of the Roosevelts had corresponded since at least 1931.[11] This federal committee, created as part of the New Deal effort to resurrect the economy and provide financial support to citizens, facilitated the federal government's purchase of supplies made by blind workers—cotton mops, corn brooms, whisk brooms, cuspidor mops, deck swabs, cocoa mats, pillowcases, triangular oil-treated mops, wall and ceiling fans, and mattresses. The invitation provided an opportunity to help implement many of the work opportunities she had advocated, work opportunities endorsed by the AFB. With the exception of the War Department, which had not dealt with her file yet, all the federal divisions had given their official nods to her appointment.[12]

Keller accepted but shortly after resigned the federal position. Writing to President Roosevelt, she explained,

> I accepted this offer with the understanding that no work would be involved. Now, however, I have learned that it would mean attending countless meetings, constant travel, detailed routine for which I have neither the professional experience nor the comprehensive knowledge required. Therefore, embarrassed and troubled as I am, I must withdraw my consent.[13]

The resignation can be interpreted to contradict her many arguments about the abilities of people with disabilities, as well as her desire to actively bring about substantive economic change for them. Still recovering emotionally from the death of Anne in 1936, and still adjusting to the assistance of someone other than Anne, however, she may not have known how to manage the obligations of a federal committee. Participating in the activities of the 1906 Massachusetts Commission for the Blind had left her and Anne Macy "breathless with the effort to keep up," and she had resolved "that never again would I allow myself to be dragged into undertakings for which I was not intended by fate." Given the past history of her political involvement and its consequences, she may have feared active participation. M. C. Migel, then president of the AFB, may have pressured her. He wrote two lengthy letters urging Keller to resign. Once he had, in her terms, "enlightened" her, she resigned and Migel was appointed in her place.[14]

Keller continued to pay close attention to the growing European conflict, especially Hitler's rise to power. She somberly read the warning notes of historian Stephen Roberts, in his 1938 book *The House that Hitler Built*.[15] That same year she also lobbied *New York Times* editor, good friend, and Westport neighbor John Finley, to devote the resources of the *Times* to publicizing the devastating situation of Jews in Nazi-occupied territory. She asked him to highlight people with disabilities—who were targeted by the Nazis as "defectives" and then denied entry into the United States and other nations because restrictive immigration laws likewise labeled them as "defectives." Both European Jews and clients and administrators of institutions for people with disabilities desperately sought help.

The other day I received a letter which, like concentrated fire, burnt deeper into my consciousness the meaning of the present crisis, for it brought the sense of a nameless shadow worse than blindness, a silence stabbed by inhumanity to defenseless handicapped fellow-beings under Nazi rulers. That is why I turn to you, Dr. Finley, a champion of the oppressed, a counselor of the bewildered. The letter is from a seeing exile who used to be an assistant at the Israelite Institute for the Blind in Vienna. Heartbroken, ashamed because she cannot use her good eyes to save others, she tells how the Nazi authorities have closed the Institute and driven out the students to beg or starve. Deliberately, as part of a ruthless, calculating scheme, these ill-starred ones—adults and children—are being reduced to misery even worse than that of Jews who can see, since blindness intensifies every privation. . . .

Unfortunately, as you are aware, it is impossible to assist these doubly stricken people individually, in view of the fact that other nations will not admit defectives to citizenship. But, Dr. Finley, is there no way in which we may hopefully approach this problem? Why we can not establish some agency private or public to create through collective action a more humane atmosphere for the Jewish blind—and the deaf too—in Austria and Germany? The letters they send me,—and oh, I receive so many!—including one from a deaf-blind poetess, are full of pathetic faith in American goodwill and counsel. They say that without any means they do not know what course to follow, but America does, and will befriend them once it is informed of their bitter plight. I wish I might lay their case before the NYT.[16]

Tragically, the 1946 fire at Keller's home at Arcan Ridge destroyed those letters. Meanwhile, in 1938, her lobbying efforts failed to bring the issue to the pages of the *New York Times*. She, however, followed her own suggestion to Finley by supporting an AFB effort to bring to the United States the head of the Vienna Jewish School for the Blind, under the guise of his learning English. In 1939, German police banned Keller's latest book, *Journal*, after she refused to delete sections expressing views favorable to Bolshevism. Lamenting Nazi restrictions on the use of Braille, she wrote to her friend Walter Holmes in 1941, "news from Europe is like a stone ever heavy upon my soul." These repeated references remind us that many in the United States were not ignorant about Nazi horrors before and during the war.[17]

In 1940, Keller served as honorary chair of the American Rescue Ship Mission. The Vichy government of France had expressed a willingness to let refugees leave concentration camps, and Latin American countries were willing to open their doors if others would pay for the refugees' transportation costs. In this effort, she sought to use her influential name to raise funds and secure the support of others such as Eleanor Roosevelt. Fears of communism, however, halted the effort to save lives. Roosevelt and others who learned of Communist support for the Mission considered that cause to reject it and notified Keller. A month later, she resigned in highly public fashion.[18]

Her comments and newspaper reportage on her resignation blamed the month-long delay on her blindness and deafness. She apologized for "staying longer than others" but explained that "on account of my handicap, I am a slow worker." Once again, newspapers and "friends" explained that political opponents had taken advantage of her disability, implying that despite fame and education, her disability rendered her politically unfit to make astute decisions. Anti-communists publicly criticized her and other members of the committee, while her file in the Military Intelligence Division of the War Department had its first entry since 1920. The incident also added weight to the "pertinent information" the Federal Bureau of Investigation kept on her. Perhaps the FBI gave her the biggest political endorsement she received after the 1920s, when it monitored her activities throughout the 1940s and 1950s. Still, the entire Rescue Ship Mission taught her a bitter lesson.[19]

Despite abhorring Nazism, Keller dreaded U.S. entry into the war. Pearl Harbor shocked her: "the thunderbolt news burst upon us that the United States is at war. My body shook like a taut rope—not from fear, I had expected it a long time, but it was an abrupt shock for me to discover that all the Japanese friends whose kindness I so gratefully remembered had been thrown into the ranks of our enemy aliens." She feared and understood the implications of Hitler but loathed the violence. She distrusted the hate-soaked nationalism of the war and knew that international tensions worked against international efforts to help people who were blind.[20]

Keller had planned to continue her international efforts and return to Japan in the early 1940s. The war in Europe had made that unlikely, but the Japanese attack on Pearl Harbor made it impossible. Simultaneously, in late 1941, AFB President M. C. Migel negotiated with the State Department's Division of Cultural Relations regarding a "Goodwill Tour" in South America (the only country specifically mentioned was Chile). The AFB had apparently proposed the trip to Keller in 1939, but at that point she instead focused on her book on Anne Sullivan. She wasn't done with the book in 1941, and wouldn't be until 1955, but she was ready to travel. Problems interfered. First, the State Department and the AFB bickered over funding.[21] Delays occurred when the State Department sought to present the matter to the Joint Congressional Committee on Cultural Relations. Migel then asked for a several month postponement. Then World War II intensified and discussion of the trip disappears from the historical record.[22]

Though the world was bleak, Helen's private world was changing for the better. Anne's 1936 death meant not only the loss of her constant companion and dearest friend but also the loss of a vibrant and provocative conversational partner. In 1903, Helen had written, "My teacher is so near to me that I scarcely think of myself apart from her." Anne's death forced Helen to re-create herself. Her sanity and happiness required new interests, cohorts, and venues of expression. An ironic result of Anne's death was that Helen's social, private, and political worlds expanded as she sought, and others sought to provide, friendship and intellectual camaraderie.[23]

Sculptor Jo Davidson was one of the most important of these friends and political dueling partners. Jo provided friendship and uncompromising access to the politics, intellectual debates, beauty, and joy of the rest of the world. For example, while the two were in Italy, he arranged for Helen to do a tactile "viewing" of Michelangelo and Donatello's sculptures. With him she debated theology, politics, art, and literature. Unlike many others, he dared to disagree with her outright and bluntly. When they spoke, she said, "his whole soul flew to his tongue." Jo characterized knowing her as "a rich adventure." Jo finger-spelled with skill, for he previously had known a deaf man who finger-spelled, and when he and Helen met in 1942, a fast friendship grew between them that required no intermediary. He was one

Jo Davidson sculpting Helen Keller in his French studio. *AP/Wide World Photos.*

of the most noted sculptors in the United States and the world and widely known for his progressive and leftist politics. The two shared a love for sculpture, Tom Paine, Walt Whitman, anti-militarism, and a passionate interest in contemporary politics that resulted in vigorous debates and frequent letters. Twice Helen sat for lengthy, intimate periods as Jo made a bust of her and a sculpture of her hands. After she turned down his repeated requests for a public endorsement of presidential candidate Henry Wallace in 1948, he responded with an assurance of continued friendship. His death in 1952 was a great loss, as his friendship had provided a venue for wide political and personal expression.[24]

After Anne died, Helen's world expanded to also include a vigorous social network emanating from Westport, Connecticut, the location of Arcan Ridge, the home to which she and Polly moved in 1939, and the New York world of Nella Braddy Henney. Both Helen and Polly also depended increasingly on Nella for business, personal, and household matters. Helen grew to love the people of these active networks and valued them for their wit, sharp opinions, and knowledge of the political world. They were important for many reasons, not the least of which was her sense of self as a politically astute person.

Take, for example, the spring of 1943. Helen spent Easter with neighbors Stuart and Sandra Grummons. There she met prison reformers, Mr. and Mrs. McCormack, and the economist Stuart Chase and his wife, author Marian Tyler. They discussed the political conditions of South America, relations between the United States and the Soviet Union, prison conditions, history, recent literature, and war resistors. Only weeks earlier she had lunched with the actress Katharine Cornell and met Countess Alexandra Tolstoy, with whom Helen said "I had all I could do to curb my argumentative tongue when the Countess spoke of Russia as if it was hopelessly lost to Christianity and civilization." Attending a New York musical and luncheon she met Austrian violinist Fritz Kreisler, who impressed her. A dinner outing in New York included Cornell's husband, the director Guthrie McClintic, actress Lillian Gish, and a Russian dissident named Koransky. Helen had apparently disagreed vehemently with McClintic and

Koransky on Soviet Russia, for her postdinner thank-you note included a three-page elaboration of her opinions on the Soviet Union. Several days later she relayed the conversation to her friend and neighbor Clare Heineman: "again I blurted out my views, that time in the presence of an unreconstructed White Russian. Alas! I am incorrigible, Clare."

When Jo and Florence Davidson visited, they brought historian Van Wyck Brooks, whose book *The Flowering of the New England Mind* Helen was reading (and who wrote a book about her in 1956). They spoke of Thoreau and Brooks's books. Saturday's guests included famed etcher Kerr Eby, *Reader's Digest* editor Mr. Waldron (she objected to its "pro-Fascist propensities"), editor Clare Booth Luce (who she didn't like because of her "anti-British 'campaign'"), and others. Helen again said proudly: "I spoke out my mind more than I intended to among some guests some of whom were strait-laced conservatives." All of this in the spring of 1943.[25]

Christmas that year was similar. She spent Christmas Day again with Stuart and Sandra Grummons. Over "a big jovial Yule-log," Helen and Stuart "settled the affairs of the universe," while they lamented the Republican Party, growing isolationism in the United States, and debated the war in Europe, the role of the Vatican in Italian politics, and Lord Macaulay's (Thomas Babington's) views on Catholic despotism.[26]

Helen loved these events. She was intensely interested in the world about her. As she wrote to Nella, her most frequent correspondent, "After the intellectual hunger I have often felt since Teacher's going it is a priceless blessing to have such friends pour manna into my desert places." These conversations and friendships provided a lifeline. In them she developed and sustained the political interests that were so vital to her own well-being. While she largely kept her interest in formal politics and her radical political analyses relatively private after the mid-1920s, they remained intense.[27]

In the midst of World War II, President Franklin Delano Roosevelt provided Keller hope. Since living in New York during his successful gubernatorial campaign, she had corresponded with him, publicly supported him, privately lobbied him on behalf of the AFB, and had met him and Eleanor several times. She agreed with him politically and felt they shared an experience of disability. Not everyone approved of her support for FDR. A letter to Nella Braddy Henney indicates that Nella and possibly people from the AFB attempted to dissuade her from voting for him in 1944. In August, Keller indicated to the *New York Times* that she would, for the first time, cast a ballot and that it would be for President Roosevelt. Why she hadn't voted before wasn't discussed and seems contrary to her political interests. In September, she wrote to Henney that "just to make sure that my 'wild, strong will' [wouldn't it be nice to know whom she was quoting?] does not run away with me and overturn the chariot of the American Foundation for the Blind. . . . I have again examined the possible consequences of casting my vote for F.D. Roosevelt, and I shall march up to the cannon's mouth just the same." She explained that she supported him because he advocated the "comprehensive policies for international cooperation out of which alone a stable, progressive world can arise." She felt him imperfect but felt he would be "at least tolerant of the labor movement." Her conscience, she insisted, "will not let me off from voting."[28]

With Jo Davidson, she attended FDR's fourth inaugural and the family's private party. It was, she felt, a somber moment: "that occasion resembled Lincoln's inaugural ceremonies. There was the same grim simplicity, the same atmosphere electric with historical and political significance." His demeanor reminded her of Cape Cod: "There was about him the same heroic endeavor to work fruitfulness and verdure out of bleak winds and bitter sands. Fearfully battered by a sea of difficulties, he stirred me with a sense of his titan resolve to wrest from it 'a better life for ourselves and all our fellowmen' and the achievement of God's will to peace on earth."[29]

Helen sought some way to aid the war effort. She participated in the development of protective measures for blind and deaf people during air raids. She then explored service as a "Gray Lady," a wartime hospital volunteer, but that never proved viable. Finally, though for most of her life she tended to avoid other people with disabilities, she and Polly spent significant time with veterans disabled by the battles of World War II.[30]

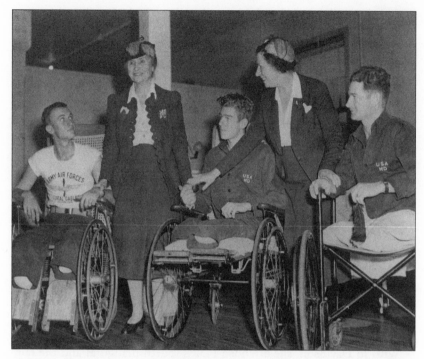

Portrait of Helen Keller, Polly Thomson, and three unidentified World War II veterans, taken during her wartime hospital tours. *Courtesy of the American Foundation for the Blind. Used with permission of the American Foundation for the Blind, Helen Keller Archives.*

These visits, however, were not made as friends and equals. Instead, Keller and others designed her visits for her to serve as a lofty and inspirational model to the men newly disabled by war. The AFB organized her lengthy hospital tours in cooperation with army and navy hospitals. In this effort, she presented two solutions to the problems posed by disability: work-oriented rehabilitation and a good attitude. Her ceaseless praise of the work-oriented rehabilitation efforts corresponded with her constant emphasis on work as an overwhelming need of people with disabilities. She argued that for all people with disabilities, but especially for veterans, work would provide economic and social usefulness. She then praised good attitudes, the aspect most highlighted by the media. She encouraged veterans to "forget the things they cannot do and think only of what they can." Their success, she argued, would be defined by their future economic usefulness and would depend on "how well their buoyancy is sustained. . . . They must be held to regard deafness not merely as a handicap, but also as an opportunity." While she emphasized work training, she rarely emphasized the job discrimination veterans would face. The media loved her veterans' hospital tours, as did the AFB, the army, and navy. The AFB publicized each of her tours of several months and in numerous states as coast-to-coast tours to "cheer blind and deaf veterans." The always unstated inference was that she served as an inspirational model to the depressed young men because of who she was *despite* her disability. From her, it was reported, the veterans "caught the spark of hope" that they too could become something *despite* their disability, if only their attitude were good enough.[31]

In a letter to Jo Davidson, Helen revealed a similar belief in 1944. She had attended an October Foreign Policy Association dinner at which FDR spoke. International politics concerned her deeply in this period, and he held her hopes for a peaceable world. Despite this, her highest compliment to the president was that she "could not realize that he was being wheeled up to the speaker's table." Rather, she "sensed his powerful spirit striding among us." In her mind's eye, she saw him "not in his wheel-chair but walking out with archangel might." To her, recognizing FDR's disability would have acknowledged a weakness that went beyond physical strength to be all encompassing. Throughout her life, she increasingly insisted that people with disabilities be considered individuals of potential, but she simultaneously considered them inherently damaged.[32]

Wrestling with her own questions about disability and purpose, Helen paid increased attention in the 1940s to other deaf-blind people, in abstract terms. Her most sympathetic ally in this effort appears to have been Walter Holmes, a long-time friend and the editor of *Matilda Ziegler Magazine*, a well-established monthly Braille publication unaffiliated with the AFB. In 1938, the two had lamented the lack of support for deaf-blind people in the United States. In 1941, they repeatedly discussed the issue in person as well as by correspondence. Holmes pursued organizational and "practical methods of assisting the doubly handicapped" and sought her assistance. She responded with enthusiasm but warned him that the AFB was unlikely "ever to find room among its many interests" for the deaf-blind. There, she wrote, "'hangs a tale' which it will be easier for me to speak than write." The lack of organizational support infuriated her. "Why cannot means be found to appoint a national council composed of workers for the blind and workers for the deaf who would meet annually and give special consideration to the problems of the deaf-blind?" Listing the American Association of Workers for the Blind, the American Society for the Hard of Hearing, and the American Association for the Teaching of Speech to the Deaf, but noticeably omitting the AFB, she wrote that the inaction of the various organizations "potently tests their sincerity towards the handicapped."[33]

"Time and time again," Helen wrote, "I have thought a champion had raised up for the large number who still live unbefriended in the double shadow of blindness and deafness, and I have been cruelly disappointed. The bitter drop must remain in my cup of blessings until a concerted effort under responsible management is made to rescue them." Her 1944 appeal to Congress to assist the deaf-blind ("the hardest pressed and least cared-for" among her "blind fellows") was only that—an appeal that went little further in the Social Security program. In 1945, she and the AFB celebrated her sixty-fifth birthday with "an educational program for the doubly afflicted on a nation-wide scale." The plan emphasized economic and personal independence as a goal and was released with the added legitimacy of a *New York Times* editorial. How this plan came about and what happened to it is unclear.[34]

In the fall of 1944, only a few weeks before her congressional appearance, Helen indicated to Nella that her advocacy for blind people had never been her primary interest.

It is perfectly true that my work for the blind is a trust, and in order to fulfill its duties justly I must keep it as the center of my external activities. But it has never occupied a center in my personality or inner relations with mankind. That is because I regard philanthropy as a tragic apology for wrong conditions under which human beings live, losing their sight or hearing or becoming impoverished, and I do not conceal this awkward position from anybody.[35]

No evidence remains that Nella commented on the matter to Helen, but it seems jarring to the contemporary reader. The comment followed Helen's insistence on voting for FDR and may have been part of her larger claim to intellectual and political independence. Her insistence that she did not "conceal this awkward position from anybody" seems self-deceiving, as there is no evidence that she expressed disillusionment with philanthropy to any of those from whom she asked money. Nor did she publicly question whether her activities, and those of philanthropists in general, addressed the fundamental issues facing blind people.

Keller's insistence on broader goals than advocacy of blind people alone, however, accords with her life's path. She had devoted the last twenty years to the AFB. As a fund-raiser and lobbyist, she succeeded, but this success had not accomplished all she sought. Anne Macy had died, and by the mid-1940s, the intense pain of her death had faded. Helen was reevaluating her life and goals and she now sought something else. "There is an even higher trust" than her work for blind people, she wrote to Nella, a trust to "keep my essential freedom so that wherever possible I may release fettered minds and imprisoned lives among the blind, let alone those who see."[36] At this point, she appears to have regarded her advocacy for people with disabilities as restrictive of her "essential freedom" and a deterrent from the larger calling of releasing "fettered minds and imprisoned lives" of all sorts.

Seeking ways to keep her "essential freedom" in the years after World War II, Keller's fund-raising and lobbying efforts on behalf of the AFB diminished. The second phase of her public political life drew to a close and she instead turned to international matters. As an international figure she remained focused on advocacy for blind people but understood her efforts to be part of a larger political agenda of world peace, the international development of human rights criteria, and the sustenance of a world community.

When FDR died in the spring of 1945, Keller had just finished greeting disabled veterans at a naval hospital and was enjoying tea with the hospital commander. It was as if, she explained to Jo Davidson, "the beneficent luminary in whose rays civilization was putting forth new leaves of healing for all people was seemingly extinguished forever. . . . All at once, a guest . . . came straight to us from the telephone with the tidings of the President's death. Everybody grew limp and silent. Soon church bells were tolling, and flags were at half-mast." FDR's death sorely tried her optimistic nature.[37]

Keller considered her extensive wartime visits with disabled U.S. soldiers important, but they did not bring her the satisfaction she sought. The vagaries of war and international politics made her even more adamant about the importance of international friendships and cooperation, even more convinced that she had an international purpose. When her Japanese friend Takeo Iwahashi reestablished contact in 1946, she called his letter "a precious confirmation of my faith through the darkest war years of history that the deep-sea cables of understanding would never snap between us despite the pain and wreckage on the surface." She eagerly sought to expand those "deep-sea cables of understanding" to other countries.[38]

Not until after the war did she travel internationally again. In concert with the Marshall Plan and U.S. efforts to provide assistance for civilians and military officials attempting to recover from the war, she went to Europe to foster support for European blind people. Her 1946 tours of war-torn Greece, Italy, France, and England took her outside of the United States, but she and others considered them an extension of wartime service. The Foundation for the Overseas Blind, part of the AFB, hoped to draw attention to the dire postwar conditions, particularly of those who were blind, and consequently raise funds in the United States. Undoubtedly, she and the AFB remembered the success of her 1943 visits to injured U.S. veterans and the institutions that serviced them. She had not looked

forward to the trip, but she cited her duty to the foundation and the appeals made directly to her. "I cannot say the prospect elates me. It will
mean heartache as I sense over there gusts from the world's distress,
famine, hope of peace deferred and international discord. But I feel a deep
necessity of going. . . . I receive constantly piteous letters from the European blind begging help, and . . . I think I can gather firsthand information
which I must have in order to lay their desperate needs before the American public effectively and raise funds for their relief." By this measure her
trip succeeded, for news reports repeatedly chronicled her appeals.[39]

Keller's 1946 tour was one of obligation and not personal satisfaction.
Postwar politics, domestic and international, irritated her. As she left, she
lamented to Henney that Harry Truman's administration, along with both
the Democratic and Republican parties, "are working towards imperialism,
and now the proof glares me in the face." She ostensibly dedicated the trip
to the blind people of war-torn Europe, but included in her visits personal
friends, international dignitaries (including Queen Elizabeth and the
pope), as well as the suffering of Europe. Her good friend Katharine Cornell had encouraged her to visit the pope, but Jo Davidson had ridiculed
the idea. The actual encounter had a comical outcome when the Holy Father mistook Polly for Helen.[40]

As a tragic finale to the trip, Helen and Polly received news that the
Arcan Ridge house had burnt to the ground. The fire destroyed everything,
including *all* of her correspondence and notes for her long-planned book
Teacher.

Once home in November 1946, Keller found her friends, supporters,
and trustees battling over the finances of rebuilding the house at Arcan
Ridge. They didn't all like one another; nor did they agree with each
other's and her politics. As she told her story of her visit with the pope
some found it hilarious while others found it sacrilegious. She also
lamented the state of U.S. politics, characterizcing it as a "bitter period of
retrograde." Home provided little pleasantness—and basically *no* home.
She and Polly stayed with various friends until the new house was completed in September 1947.[41]

In February 1947, Keller tried to battle that retrograde by endorsing David Lilienthal's nomination as chair of the Atomic Energy Commission. Lilienthal opposed continued atomic weapons development and proposed that an international body be established to monitor research on atomic energy in the hopes of avoiding rivalry between nations. The growing Red Scare and accusations of Communist sympathies made the approval of his nomination increasingly unlikely. Jo and Nella also supported Lilienthal. Recognizing her cultural weight, Nella, Polly Thomson, and Helen "all piled over to Jo's. . . . It was decided that Helen would write a letter to the Times." The resulting letter was classic Helen Keller and began with a statement of self: "As a free citizen and a thinking daughter of democracy I am moved to speak my mind in the present conflict between light and darkness." The campaign against Lilienthal, she said, was a "conscienceless campaign of political goring and tossing."[42]

The goring of the presidential election also caught Keller's attention. In 1948, she considered endorsing Henry Wallace's presidential campaign. Wallace had excited and inspired her when they had met at a 1944 rally for Roosevelt. After FDR's death, she characterized the Truman administration as "an uninspired, short-sighted administration [that] has made havoc of the farseeing, beneficent global policies for which he [FDR] gave his life." When Truman fired Wallace in September 1946 from his position as secretary of agriculture, she expressed continued alarm about the United States and the world in the wake of World War II. She regretted that she and "the American people" had been "ignominiously slow about supporting Wallace in his struggle to check the disgraceful squabbles between the supposed Allies and restore F.D.R.'s magnanimous foreign policy as a counselor and friend of mankind." She held Truman partially responsible for increasing racial discrimination, the hunting and stifling of radicals and liberals, and increased militarism and atomic development.[43]

Jo Davidson, who Helen loved and depended on for political conversation, led much of the national effort for Wallace's presidency in 1948. He attempted to involve her in the Independent Citizens' Committee of Arts, Sciences and Professions, formerly an organization of FDR allies that now supported Wallace. Accusations of communism smeared Jo's name and he sought new names to lead the Wallace campaign. Helen appeared prominently in a March 1947 Madison Square Garden rally for Wallace, apparently thrilled by Wallace, the cheering crowd of 19,000, and numerous celebrities. She sat on the stage with honor and was the first to embrace Wallace after his speech.[44]

Everyone had ideas about what Keller should do regarding Wallace. Nella noted in her journal that "Helen's is the one he [Jo] wants, but every word he said convinced me more and more that hers is the name he must not have." The AFB, Nella, and Katharine ("Kit") Cornell warned her that publicly supporting Wallace was dangerous in the growingly rabid anti-Communist atmosphere. It also made fund-raising on behalf of the AFB difficult. This was born out in an attack on her politics and political allies in the nationally syndicated column of Westbrook Pegler.[45] AFB donations went down, and AFB leader Robert Irwin warned her that her interests might cause the House Un-American Affairs Committee to investigate the foundation. He then had a letter sent to contributors, reassuring them of Helen's patriotism and declaring that "naturally some of the Socialistic and Communistic leaders have taken advantage of her interest in the humanitarian side of their professings." Irwin expressed the AFB's concern about her politics more bluntly in a letter to AFB President William Ziegler: "Helen Keller's habit of playing around with Communists or near-Communists has long been a source of embarrassment to her conservative friends." The pressure against her participation in the Wallace campaign was, as Nella characterized it, "tremendous."[46]

Simultaneous with all of this, while still homeless and only two months after arriving home in late 1946, Helen began plans for another international trip. She eagerly prepared for an almost year-long trip to visit Australia, New Zealand, Japan, India, Pakistan, Egypt, Iran, Iraq, Syria, Lebanon, and Palestine. She planned a three-month stay in Japan, and Iwahashi had secured the preliminary approval of General Douglas MacArthur, Supreme Commander for the Allied Powers and the de facto ruler of Japan during the years of U.S. occupation. She told Migel, "I have a strong feeling that if the tour is marshaled with skill and energy . . . Polly and I will be factors in a movement of tremendous benefit to the twelve million blind who live in intellectual darkness."[47]

MacArthur was powerful, but Migel held the purse-strings and said no. AFB officials worried about Keller's health and even enlisted her brother Phillip to dissuade her. Close friends worried about Polly's health, not Helen's. A month later she tried again: "Please forgive me if I again take up the question of my going to the Orient which we discussed last Wednesday. It lies heavy upon my heart, and will not let me rest. . . . I cannot relinquish the dream easily. I feel a force drawing me to them that I cannot define, and when a call is disobeyed, you know, Mr. Migel, that one's peace of mind is profoundly disturbed." God called her, she insisted, "to reach the blind of the world as soon as possible." She and Polly, she insisted further, were not "afraid of hard conditions. . . . We do not fear an agitated state of affairs in China or India." Appealing even further, she wrote, "As a friend of the blind, I implore you to cooperate with me in this supreme wish of my life." Migel gave in and preparations for the 1948 trip began in earnest.[48]

For Keller, the trip signified a new, purposeful, and expanded focus on the world's blind people. After a ten-year interruption, she could begin to fulfill the international agenda she had only begun to define with the 1937 trip to Japan. Before she left she wrote to Jo, telling him that she could not lend her name to the Wallace presidential campaign. She explained that she could not do the thorough examination of Wallace she desired. Her limited energy must be targeted toward the world's blind people. She could not, she told him, carry on "two or more diverse kinds of work at once." The citizenship she sought, one in which she could act on multiple political interests, was nearly impossible. Furthermore, the "great problems of the earth" depended on "the rising good sense and strength of mankind," and not the actions of the United States. The same was true for "the problems of the blind throughout the world." It was thus her job to encourage the goodness of humanity and highlight the needs of blind people globally.

Unless each country is aroused to a sense of its duties towards them, all the progress that America has made towards their liberation is futile. I will do my best, wherever I go, to give a message for the blind struggling with their local environment which varies from land to land, and when at last true civilization dawns, society will safeguard their liberties and rights.[49]

Keller enjoyed New Zealand and Australia, but Japan became the heart of the 1948 trip. More than anything else, her successful Japanese tour convinced her that she had the skills to fulfill the international agenda she had tentatively embraced with her 1937 trip to Japan. The enthusiastic reception given her by the Japanese public, the thrilled response of the U.S. government to this reception, the intensity with which she enjoyed the trip, and the profound unease generated in her by Hiroshima and Nagasaki, called her to international action.

U.S. military personnel were apparently lukewarm at best about the arrival of a sixty-eight-year-old deaf-blind woman they presumed to be exhausted after two months of travel. Expectations of Keller's debilitated nature had been similar in Australia where, according to Nella Braddy Henney, "knowing of Helen's afflictions, they were prepared for almost anything in the way of helplessness, physical grotesqueness and unpleasantness. As soon as Polly had Helen's hand firmly on the railing of the gangplank she turned her loose to make the descent alone while she herself concluded some minor business with one of the officials on the ship. . . . Helen always descends stairs alone and does everything else she can alone. But arriving there in Sydney and coming down the gangplank with her light, free step and her radiant smile, she seemed like a goddess."[50]

The similarly erroneous expectations of U.S. military personnel in Japan resulted in a comic arrival in Japan. Henney reported that the military officials from SCAP, the Supreme Commander for the Allied Powers, assigned to watch over Polly Thomson and Keller spent the night before their coming bewailing "the arrival of two doddering females, two old hags." Military officials even arranged for an unneeded ambulance to await the pair.

They escorted Keller and Thomson to tea but ended up securing Scotch, Keller's drink of choice. Their travelmates, Dr. Milton T. Stauffer and his wife, affiliated with the religiously based John Milton Society for the Blind, provided another complication. According to Henney, the couple had "already got into the hair of the military." This was apparently meant quite literally, for Dr. Stauffer said something about hair to the nearly bald General MacArthur, who felt very sensitive about that matter. The occupation forces "hadn't liked them." Numbers made the entourage bulky. As a result, Keller, Thomson, Takeo Iwahashi and his wife Keo, and Lane Carlson of the U.S. forces traveled together while the Stauffers went in a separate direction.[51]

SCAP official Lane Carlson apparently grew to enjoy the pair greatly. As Henney characterized the relationship, "Lane learned, as many others have learned, that it is not merely edifying to travel around with Helen and Polly . . . it is fun. It has always been fun to be with them. . . . Lane's first letter to the Old Hags after they came back to the US began 'Precious li'l chickens.'"[52]

In 1948, the postwar U.S. occupational force dominated Japan, as it had and as it would. Earlier that year, the number of U.S. officials peaked at 3,200, even though the six year occupation was only half completed. The United States sought to remake Japan structurally, governmentally, economically, socially, and psychologically. As historian John Dower observes the period, it is "difficult to find another cross-cultural moment more intense, unpredictable, ambiguous, confusing and electric than this one."[53]

Some Japanese citizens anticipated that Keller's visit could bring renewal. Takeo Iwahashi hoped she would bring funds and rekindle efforts to aid Japanese blind people, particularly in the devastated postwar physical and economic conditions. One man, who had met her during her 1937 visit, wrote, "The greater part of Japanese strive with great pains for recovering from 'Severe Wounds of hearts'. . . . For this reason, *I am on the tiptoe of expectation* that your visit to Japan again shall give us the brightest light" [italics added].[54]

Many Japanese citizens responded to Keller similarly. Her open address at the Imperial Palace, according to one report, drew a crowd of fifty thousand. Other accounts put the number at seventy thousand, some set it as high as 300,000. Crowds lined the streets wherever she went. She met Emperor Hirohito and Empress Nagako, as well as General Douglas MacArthur. Iwahashi estimated that in her visits with government officials, U.S. army groups, private groups, and at public meetings, the number of people who came to see her "would easily top 2 million." The *Mainichi Press*, an English-language newspaper, sponsored the Helen Keller Campaign Committee, which raised over 100 million yen for aid to blind people, many of them blinded by the war. The Campaign Committee sponsored an official "Helen Keller song" composed for the occasion.[55]

During her trip, Keller constantly preached the need for action on behalf of blind (and sometimes deaf) people. She called on social workers in Osaka to go beyond the counsel and assistance of the U.S. government and to "take initiative" in the "cause of the blind and deaf." She told the women of Japan, "who are advancing so wonderfully to a wide national usefulness," that they had a unique role in "work for the blind." Women should "include among the objects of your special love and aid the blind and the deaf and all whose eyes or ears are threatened." She urged that social service agencies train blind women for employment as teachers of music, language, mathematics, history, literature, geography, and Braille, as well as concert musicians, physiotherapists, stenographers, switchboard operators. She encouraged blind women to seek these positions. Such advice must have sounded otherworldly to Japanese women struggling with malnutrition and survival.[56]

Keller remained relatively quiet in public about the personally most profound aspect of her trip. On October 13 and 14, 1948, she visited Hiroshima and Nagasaki, the sites of massive U.S. atomic attacks. She arrived in Hiroshima first, planning to make her usual appeal for funds and support. In her public speech she acknowledged the "cruel nemesis that overtook" the city but told its citizens that tragedy "generated new forces of

Helen Keller and Polly Thomson in Nagasaki, Japan, 1948. *Courtesy of the American Foundation for the Blind. Used with permission of the American Foundation for the Blind, Helen Keller Archives.*

Polly Thomson, Helen Keller, and unidentified U.S. military personnel in Japan, 1948. *Courtesy of the American Foundation for the Blind. Used with permission of the American Foundation for the Blind, Helen Keller Archives.*

Helen Keller and Polly Thomson in Fukuoka, Japan, 1948. *Courtesy of the American Foundation for the Blind. Used with permission of the American Foundation for the Blind, Helen Keller Archives.*

Polly Thomson and Helen Keller in Nagoya, Japan, 1948. Note Keller lip-reading Polly Thomson before the huge crowd. *Courtesy of the American Foundation for the Blind. Used with permission of the American Foundation for the Blind, Helen Keller Archives.*

healing." The new Japan espoused by the United States provided the solution and the redemption, "The new sense you are gaining of personal freedom and responsibility for the welfare of others and your adoption of the
principles and practices of democracy. Then truly will your tragedy be a
purification of your souls through public spirit and brotherhood."[57]

Privately, Helen said more to Nella, who then forwarded the letter to Jo.
"We are still aching all over from that piteous experience—it exceeds in
horror and anguish the accounts I have read," she wrote. "Polly and I went
to Hiroshima with Takeo Iwahashi to give our usual appeal meeting, but
no sooner had we arrived than the bitter irony of it all gripped us overpow-
eringly, and it cost us a supreme effort to speak."[58]

Helen had visited the city in 1937 and found the difference unimagin-
able. "Instead of the fair, flourishing city we saw eleven years ago, there is
only life struggling daily, hourly against a bare environment, unsoftened
even by nature's wizardry. How the people exist through summer heat and
winter cold is a thought not to be borne." The human misery was more
than she knew how to communicate.

> Jolting over what had once been paved streets, we visited the one grave—
> all ashes—where about 8:30, August 6, 1945, ninety thousand men,
> women and children were instantly killed, and a hundred and fifty thou-
> sand were injured, and the rest of the population did not know at the
> moment what an ocean of disaster was upon them . . . the flash of light
> that brought mass death. As a result of that inferno two hundred thou-
> sand persons are now dead, and the suffering caused by atomic burns
> and other wounds is incalculable. Polly saw burns on the face of the wel-
> fare officer—a shocking sight. He let me touch his face, and the rest is si-
> lence—the people struggle on and say nothing about their lifelong
> hurts.[59]

Helen and Polly visited the city's Peace Tower and the park intended to
be a memorial to the bombing. She wrote to Nella that the "unsmiling silence" of the people around her "seemed to call for a word of comfort." In

her public speech, she encouraged Hiroshima's residents that "by adopting the principles and practices of true democracy it [the city] would attain a higher greatness, and the Tower rising before us above the desolation was a challenging evidence that Hiroshima was leading Nippon in the way of disarmament and good-will." Several days afterward she learned "with deep humility how touched the people of Hiroshima were by my few words, and as a result they are trying to put up a bell on the Peace Tower which will ring to remind the city of its new mission." Privately, she wrote to Nella, "I left with a conviction that the splendor of a genuine victory would belong to Hiroshima, not to America."[60]

For Helen, the city of Nagasaki also "scorched a deep scar in my soul." She and Polly walked through "the mangled corpse of one of Japan's beneficent enterprises—the medical college and the clinic where the patients were killed by the bomb." The pair "stumbled over ground cluttered in every direction like foundation-stones, timbers, broken pipe-lines, bits of machinery and twisted girders. I felt sure that I smelt the dust from the burning of Nagaski—the smoke, of death." Helen met Takashi Nagai, a physician and scientist who had survived the attack, but now lay dying of radiation sickness. "Yes, Nella," Helen wrote, "Polly saw him dying with her own eyes, and was almost unable to speak or spell." The famed Christian, widowed by the attack, wrestled with the meaning of the devastation. His books reflected on his imminent death, on what would happen to his young children, on the future of Japan, and on the attack's theological significance. Like many others, Helen visited his deathbed in a small iron hut near the center of the explosion. Her visit, almost a pilgrimage, further cemented the man's reputation as the "saint of Nagasaki."[61]

As Helen left Japan, unexpectedly only ten days later, she thanked the "so frightfully shattered" cities of Hiroshima and Nagasaki for the way they "poured gifts upon us as sunbeams out of their ruin and anguish." Privately, she wrote to Nella of the discomfort the enthusiastic reception had given her. "Despite the consummate barbarity of some military forces of my country and the painful wreckage upon the survivors," Japanese citizens listened to her. Along with an "affectionate welcome," "gifts were poured upon us out of the people's destitution and sorrow." Of the gifts, she wrote, "My pain made me almost mute, but I managed to tell the Governor, the Mayor and other representatives of the welcoming committee that a city [Hiroshima] which has such magnificent will to give cannot really perish." Such generosity of spirit, she wrote, "will remain in my soul, a holy memory—and a reproach."[62]

The devastation of the atomic attacks strengthened her commitment to international cooperation. She felt herself and her nation reproached and sought absolution. She described herself to Nella as "more determined than ever to do what lies in my power to fight against the demons of atomic warfare and for the constructive uses of atomic energy." The trip grounded her previous opinions in personal experience: "For many years I have sensed profoundly the war-made wrongs and crookedness of mankind, but now it is more than a feeling, it is a concrete knowledge I have gained and a stern resolve to work for the breaking of barbarism and the fostering of universal peace."[63]

The trip also had physical consequences for both women. Polly's health had previously been fragile, and it should be no surprise that her blood pressure caused the trip to come to an end only days later. Helen wrote to Nella that "Polly says there has never been such revolt in her soul before, and life will not be the same for her after Hiroshima and Nagasaki." Nella later saw newsreel film of the two in Hiroshima and noted, "Helen's face—angry, stern, shocked—at Hiroshima is something to remember."[64]

Keller's rich description of the cities and their people leaves no question about the depth of her ability to perceive or to "know." Since *The Story of My Life* (1903), critics had maligned her use of visual imagery, arguing that she had no direct access to visual knowledge. By using such literary devices, she not only wrote in the language in which she read, however, but also claimed an authorial position which hid her disability. In Mary Klages's analysis, Keller used visual imagery to convey "subjective meanings, referring to moods or emotions" rather than just the visual. In this case, her use of nonvisual descriptors is profound. She describes the uneven ground, the mangled remnants of buildings, the lingering smell, the melted face of a fellow human being, the overwhelming solemnity and weight of a grave of ninety thousand, and conversations with those who knew they were dying.[65]

Regarding Hiroshima and Nagasaki, the contrast between Helen's public and private statements is marked. She publicly praised democracy as the solution to Japan's problems but privately lamented that the bomb "summons our democracies to the bar of Judgment." The contrast reveals her unease with making public statements of political importance in this period. It reflects her affirmed and newly adamant conviction that war is wrong, and her belief that she should and could do something about international hostilities. It also reveals her understandable inability to comprehend and make sense of the devastation caused by her own country. Never again would she think of U.S. military force nor her international citizenry in the same manner. In her words, "the splendor of a genuine victory would belong to Hiroshima, not to America." Hiroshima shook her understanding of the place of the United States in the world and caused her to question U.S. rightness. Publicly, however, she remained silent.[66]

One wonders if Keller remembered her earlier response to 1946 bomb experiments at Bikini Island. In July of that year, she had sat around the radio with friends, in "a whirlwind of excitement." As she had described to her friend Clare Heineman, "An appalling silence followed until my fingers on the radio diaphragm caught the quite distinct vibrations of the plane which dropped the bomb, the death-boding whistles and the suspense for which there is no name. It was like the Day of Judgement—and in a sense it really is—a verdict being passed upon a mighty age and a diapason of world events announcing the entry of an even more stupendous era. How amazing it all is!"[67]

The Japanese received Helen with almost universal praise. The editors of *The (Tokyo) Mainichi* paid tribute to her efforts, telling her that all of Japan had been given "great spiritual encouragement by your holy efforts. We firmly believe it is not exaggeration to say that you brought to this country the most effective and ceaseless spiritual stimulation since the termination of the war." The Osaka Municipal Assembly expressed similar sentiments, thanking her for visiting Japan, despite "an advanced age, and triple physical handicaps." A teacher at the Nara School for the Blind, who had seen her while a student at the Tokyo School for the Blind in 1937, wrote, "I felt a deep impression when I shook hands with you at Nara station, you were leaving for Kyoto. I cannot forget the scene forever. I thank you very much." Even in 1959, a Japanese legislator sent notice of a bill he expected to be passed imminently, which provided funds for people with disabilities, and offered his "deepest gratitude" for "the boundless assistance of love you have rendered my country for many years past."[68]

When Helen arrived in Hiroshima, Mayor Shinzo Hamai told her that she represented "the greatness of striving by having overcome a threefold handicap. We of Hiroshima are now striving to follow the path that you have trodden." U.S. military official Laurence Critchell analyzed Keller's broad appeal as one of hope. The Japanese, he argued, had for centuries "accepted their misfortunes. They had endured poverty, illness, malnutrition, famine, earthquake, typhoons and wars. They had resigned themselves; the misery of their lives was way beyond remedy. Now they had a new hope. . . . And the symbol of it . . . was Miss Helen Keller—who had not just accepted deafness, who had not just accepted a mute tongue, but who had learned to see, to hear, to speak, and to fill every human heart who saw her with pride in the human spirit." Her ability to "overcome" blindness and deafness was embraced as a model for postwar Japan. For Japanese citizens and their U.S. conquerors, her disability served literally and metaphorically to embody the devastation of war; her successful life was proof that the impossible was possible.[69]

Everything halted late in October 1948 when Polly's health faltered seriously. U.S. General Crawford Sams of the occupying forces ordered the trip cut short, ending plans for Polly and Helen to journey to Korea, China, Burma, Egypt, Iran, India, Pakistan, Palestine, Siam, and Turkey. Helen regretted leaving but understood the seriousness of Polly's health problems. As she sailed home, she wrote to her host General Sams that she regretted "that we had not carried out the world tour to which we had dedicated our best endeavors as a climax of our loves, but, as I look back over the past two months, I find comfort in the seeds of constructive good that are being sown on fertile soil for the handicapped of Japan."[70]

The State Department noted Keller's success immediately. Before she left Japan, the U.S. ambassador to the Philippines invited her to visit the Philippines. (Secretary of State George C. Marshall had been working on the effort since at least June.) The ambassador praised her, saying that her trip to Japan "is one in which the Department is very much interested. The United States could not have a better ambassador of good will than yourself, for your interest in and inspiration to people in all parts of the world transcend national barriers in a way that does honor to you and to your country." The Philippines had just acquired its independence and the U.S. government sought to assure it of "our continued interest in them." Helen Keller was apparently a way to do so. The 1948 trip to Japan solidified Keller's standing with the State Department and the AFB as a worthy and effective ambassador of U.S. culture and ideals. It also strengthened her conviction that the world needed her, and that she had the skills to respond.[71]

4

I Will Not Allow
Polly to Climb
a Pyramid

1948–1968

I will not allow Polly to climb a pyramid. . . . But I shall
climb one with Mr. Meyer.
                            —Helen Keller, 1952, age 72 years

The numerous international trips Helen Keller made between 1937 and 1948, especially the 1948 trip to Japan, began a rich international life and transformed her from a tourist into an ambassador. From that point forward, she traveled abroad, in a semiofficial ambassadorial status, virtually every other year until 1957, at which point the seventy-seven-year-old woman retired from international travel.

These same trips, especially again her 1948 trip to Japan, also established her with the State Department as a weighty and effective symbol of Americanism. State Department officials clearly recognized her as a political asset. Though her 1948 trip was not under the official auspices of the State Department, the department assisted by providing publicity materials (photographs, publications, press biographies) and asked all the various U.S. embassies involved to provide "all such courtesies . . . as befit a person of her outstanding character." U.S. ambassadors began to request her. For example, even though her original itinerary did not include Turkey, the U.S. ambassador there requested of the secretary of state that she visit. The State Department assisted in the change of plans, even though it took pains to remind officials that she was not "under the auspices of the Department." In a letter stamped "restricted," the State Department noted that "the prestige of the U.S. cannot but be advanced by assisting Miss Keller to receive as favorable an introduction as possible to the peoples of the countries she and her party may visit."[1]

The AFB remained officially in charge of Keller's international travel, but the State Department became increasingly involved throughout the 1950s. Her interests in travel and global cooperation neatly coincided with the federal government's interests in promoting U.S. influence in the cold war battle against the Soviet Union. The State Department thus devoted significant energy to easing and publicizing her travel schedule and her persona as a representative of Americanism. For the State Department, her international success served as a huge boon.

Keller's international travel also neatly coincided with her religious faith, allowing her to blend her theological interests in service and universal salvation. In *My Religion* (1927), she chronicled her theological wrestlings with the argument that those who did not believe in Christ, regardless of their goodness, were doomed to hell. She grew to believe instead that "God has 'other sheep who hear his voice and obey him' (John 10:16). He has provided religion of some kind everywhere, and it does not matter to what race or creed people belong if they are faithful to their ideals of right living. The one principle to be remembered by all is that religion is to live a doctrine, not merely to believe one." She listed Mohammed as an example of how God "has never left Himself without a witness." Religious creed thus did not have to separate people committed to "right living." Combining this belief in universalism with her commitment to service personally and religiously compelled her to act internationally.[2]

It also appears that Keller did not want to stay home for long. Polly's health had cut the 1948 trip short, causing her to miss India, Pakistan, Egypt, Iran, Iraq, Syria, Lebanon, and Palestine. In the spring of 1950, they made a personal trip to Europe, spending time with Jo and Florence Davidson in France and Italy. Jo made special arrangements for Helen to touch sculptures of Donatello and Michelangelo. She also sat for another sculpting and the two friends spoke of plans to visit Israel together. Re-

Table 1 Keller's international travel on behalf of the AFB.

Country	Year of visit	Country	Year of Visit
Australia	1948	Jordan	1947, 1952
Brazil	1953	Korea	1937
Canada	1957	Lebanon	1947, 1952
Chile	1953	Mexico	1953
Denmark	1957	Manchuria	1937
Egypt	1947, 1952	New Zealand	1948
England	1930, 1932, 1933, 1946, 1947	Norway	1957
Finland	1957	Palestine	1957
France	1931, 1946, 1952, 1956	Panama	1953
Greece	1946	Philippines	1955
Hong Kong	1955	Peru	1953
Iceland	1957	Scotland	1930, 1932, 1933
India	1955	South Africa	1951
Ireland	1930, 1946	Sweden	1957
Israel	1952	Switzerland	1957
Italy	1946	Syria	1947, 1952
Jamaica	1935	The Vatican	1946
Japan	1937, 1948, 1955	Yugoslavia	1931–32

turning home in July, she wrote her thanks: "Our discussions over a glass of wine and hors d'oeuvre or at tea-time or dinner about human nature, freedom, art and the nemesis of the Roman Catholic Church were to me a mine of independent thinking." She loved their disagreements and his intellectual offerings. For her, he had secured Braille copies of Anatole France's *L'ile des Pingouins* and *La Revolte des Anges*, as well as Voltaire's *Candide*. "It was more than I could have hoped," she wrote, "having you there while I read them and hearing your comments upon their significance and their influence upon France."[3]

Only two months later, in September, while Jo stayed in Europe to escape McCarthyism, Herbert Haas died. Haas had served as the household caretaker since 1936. Polly and Helen loved and depended on him. When Helen wrote to Jo about his death, she described not only the loneliness that had descended on the household but also referred obliquely to the question of who was going to perform his former tasks, such as lawn-work, snow shoveling, shopping, and general household maintenance. Herbert's death made more difficult the already complex household arrangements. Nella, other friends, and Helen's trustees worried almost constantly about what would happen when Polly died. Polly's niece Effie tried to join the household, but the new relationships didn't work. Helen, Polly, and the trustees wrangled over Helen's annual income and how it would cover household help. Life in the United States, domestic politics, world events, her role in the AFB, and household affairs made Helen increasingly uneasy and dissatisfied.[4]

The AFB and AFB leaders needed Keller and cared for her but continued to have misgivings about her politically. For example, in November 1950, the AFB's Executive Director Robert Barnett expressed frustration with her politics. As the AFB prepared to give her an award in 1951, it sought an equally respected and renowned woman to speak. Keller and Eleanor Roosevelt had known each other since the early 1930s. In the postwar period, lists of the world's most admired women frequently included both, both became spokespersons on behalf of internationalism and international alliances, and both shared the experience of becoming strong international figures after the death of the primary person in their lives (Anne Macy and FDR). In the 1950s, they were not intimate friends but shared some of the same social circles. The combination of the two women, Barnett felt, would provide "a very neat publicity package along the line of one feminine world citizen and leader honoring another feminine world citizen and leader." At the same time, however, the AFB, which had been doing all it could to contain Keller's political views, feared that its members and donors had "personal reactions to the name of Eleanor Roosevelt."[5]

Keller was already making plans to leave her complicated domestic affairs again and to visit South Africa. Rev. Arthur Blaxall, a member of the Southern African National Council for the Blind and an acquaintance since 1931, extended the formal invitation. Nella Henney encouraged

Helen to be wary of Polly Thomson's health: "Think long and hard before you make any decision about South Africa." Barnett did all he could to encourage the trip. Keller's personal preparations were intense for she was acutely aware of the intensifying racial apartheid of South Africa. She read Alan Paton's *Cry the Beloved Country*, a novel critiquing his homeland's racial divisions, and Mahatma Gandhi's *Autobiography*. Her friends Mathilde and Robert Pfeiffer introduced her to a scientist familiar with the people, plants, and animals of South Africa.[6] Most striking for her was a multifaceted evening in Harlem at which she learned "the historic point of view." As she often did, she told it all to Jo Davidson. Rev. Dr. Adam Clayton Powell, Sr., minister at the Abyssinian Baptist Church, one of the largest and most dynamic congregations in Harlem, and his wife had invited her to "the colored debutantes' cotillion." There she conversed intensely with guest of honor Ralph Bunche, the first person of African descent to be awarded the Nobel Peace Prize (1950, only months previously), a leading U.S. expert on African and colonial affairs, and a fierce advocate of decolonization. Keller reflected seriously on Bunche's description of South Africa's racial divisions and the miserable conditions of black workers.[7]

She wanted to confront the racism of South African society directly but felt she had to be very careful. According to her biographer Joseph Lash, before leaving the United States in February 1951, she sent her intended speech to her host Arthur Blaxall, whom she considered an advocate of racial equality. She wrote that she sought "skill and tact as well as enthusiasm to obtain the right help for the colored blind, who, owing to their handicap are more subject to the arbitrary will of white society than their seeing fellows." Blaxall approved. At a news conference immediately prior to her departure, she mentioned the racial disparities among the opportunities available for blind peoples but focused on drums and zebras (the zebras she would encounter at Kruger National Park). Newspaper reportage noted that she "radiated enthusiasm" as she spoke of her desire to "catch glimpses of the tribal life and of the great hills and wonderful plains. To me it is all novel and full of enchantment."[8]

The trip's schedule was intense. Accompanied by AFB staffer Alfred Allen and Polly she visited twenty-eight schools and institutions, addressed forty-eight meetings and receptions, toured national parks and Victoria Falls, and visited every major urban center. In Natal, she met Mahatma Gandhi's daughter. Huge crowds greeted her wherever she went. As her host Blaxall noted, "for two months she was the center of interests, and a subject of conversation, eclipsing even the parliamentary news of the day." Racial segregation contributed to the frenzied schedule. As she described to her Japanese friend Takeo Iwahashi upon her return home, "We held three or four meetings almost every day, which was part of the racial problem. The whites, the colored people, the Indians and the natives refuse to assemble in the same places."[9]

Keller criticized racial apartheid publicly and privately. On a basic level, by addressing audiences of nonwhites she explicitly acknowledged their worth. According to a South African newspaper, an address to a white audience included "concern about the thousands of natives who were as yet untaught and unbefriended." A personal account of her trip published in Cape Town included her statement that "again and again I have witnessed the failure of society to redeem the blind and the deaf simply because of racial prejudice—an offense against humanitarianism which life never forgives." In honor of her efforts, an African group gave her the name *Nomvuselelo* (Zulu) *Matsoseletso* (Sotho), meaning "You have aroused the consciences of many."[10]

Keller felt unsure that she had sufficiently aroused the conscience of anyone, but she kept her strongest opinions on the country and its race relations private. To Takeo Iwahashi, she insisted that she had "worked with all my strength" to plead for more schools and workshops for "the colored and the native handicapped," but feared that apartheid compromised the welfare of most of South Africa's blind and deaf citizens. As nearly always, she addressed her strongest and most considered opinions to her dear friend Jo Davidson. The omnipresent "bitter racialism" clashed with the beautiful South African countryside. It took "all the courage and fortitude Polly and I could command" to make public pleas for education and em-

Keller with Zulu tribes people in South Africa, 1951. *Corbis. © Bettmann/CORBIS. Used with permission.*

ployment for the indigenous blind and deaf people. Frustration caused her to have dreams of "bang[ing] my head against an impenetrable wall trying to find a breakthrough." She wrote that her "mutinous lips"—the result of her repugnance for South Africa's racial divisions—often made convincing those with money in South African society to improve the conditions for *all* of South Africa's blind people difficult. While at Radcliffe in 1900, she had written a college paper describing white South Africans as "the heroic Boers." Clearly, by the time she returned to the United States in August 1951, she had changed her mind.[11]

Helen and Polly had not been home long before they and others began active preparations for additional foreign travel. Enthralled for years by Jo's descriptions of and passion for Israel, Helen had long wanted to visit the new country. According to Nella, the John Milton Society for the Blind and the American Federation for Overseas Blind (AFOB, the newly re-named international arm of the AFB) wanted Helen to visit Iran and Iraq. Jo died in early January 1952, and Helen may have seen a trip to the region as a testimony to her good friend, just as she had understood the 1937 trip to Japan as a testimony to Anne. The trip also allowed Helen to ignore con-tinued domestic tensions. Nella and others largely blamed Polly for the constant turnover in household help but also worried about Polly's health. Nella and their new friend Nancy Hamilton thought the pair lonely. The resulting escape was a three-month expedition to Egypt, Syria, Lebanon, Jordan, and Israel planned for the spring of 1952.[12]

Tensions between the newly created Israel and its neighboring countries complicated the politics of the journey. The State Department gave its ap-proval with the stipulation that Keller visit Israel last. With an Israeli entry visa stamp on her passport she would not have been able to enter any Arab country. Money also threatened to derail the trip. Jo assisted before his death, persuading the Israeli government and U.S. lawyer Bartley Crum to assist with travel expenses.[13]

Polly, Nella, and Helen prepared for the trip in different ways. Nella thought Helen "naturally antagonistic to the Arabs." She blamed Jo and Florence Davidson and Bartley Crum for "so ably and emotionally" advo-cating Israel and complained that "people are inclined to forget the un-happiness and misery of the dispossessed Arabs." To counter this, Nella convinced a friend "to line some up for Helen before she leaves." Helen read up on Middle Eastern politics, with and without Nella's help, and worked on speeches. She resolved emphatically that Polly would not be al-lowed to climb pyramids but decided she herself would. Polly had the re-sponsibility of gathering adequate books and clothing. As was increasingly common, Nella worried about the two. As she wrote to their friends Philip and Lenore Smith upon their April 1952 departure, "Both girls were *very* tired when they left. . . . I think it is because deep in her heart she [Polly] knows how dangerous a chance she is taking in going so far alone with Helen. . . . The program is murderous and I shall be very troubled until they are safe at home again."[14]

The State Department also prepared for Keller's trip, which came under the purview of the Near Eastern Affairs/Policy Division (NEA/P). State Department files note that the government was "most favorably impressed with the possibilities in the tour." Secretary of State Dean Acheson wrote to regional diplomatic officers that the visit should be "publicized as an example of American interest and friendship with the Near East." Photographs and materials on Keller published in Arabic were sent by diplomatic pouch.[15]

Washington officials at first sought to limit news regarding the planned stop in Israel. The State Department told embassy personnel in Egypt, Syria, Lebanon, and Jordan to keep publicity regarding the Israel stop "to a minimum." The State Department planned for the entourage to wait to acquire Israeli visas until 72 hours before their arrival. The second vital detail was the financial arrangements of the flights. The AFOB had limited finances and hoped not to spend them on airfare. Involving more arms of government, the State Department lobbied the Civil Aeronautics Board (CAB) to grant TWA and Pan Am permission to provide free transportation. Keller's trip, a State Department official wrote, "will be appreciated by the peoples and governments of the Near East as another example of the goodwill of the American people and Government. . . . in furtherance of United States foreign policy."[16]

After the CAB denied the free flights, officials from the Near Eastern Affairs/Policy Division of the State Department recruited William Thorp, assistant secretary of state, to pressure the chair of the CAB with only two weeks left before the departure date. Thorp acknowledged that the State Department should not tell the CAB what to do, but he said this was a circumstance with "a strong showing of national interest" that would not occur without free transport. Keller's previous travel had produced results. "The favorable response among the peoples whom she visited was so pronounced that the national good will engendered thereby was definitely very great. Her trip this time is expected to be fully as effective in building up good will." He asked that the CAB reconsider. Though the CAB was not convinced, Keller secured flights and left the country presumably at AFOB expense.[17]

Egypt was the first stop. Over the almost two weeks Helen and Polly spent as guests of the Egyptian government in April 1952, they visited schools for blind children, a sphinx, pyramids, schools for deaf children, and the American College for Girls, as well as lecturing at American University. Helen cited tea at the Feminist Union as a favorite event. The Egyptian women were "charming," she wrote Nella, "progressive in their ideas, with whom it was a delight to discuss various aspects of history and who, I believe, will exercise a potent influence on the higher development of their country." She "pleaded" with government ministers to establish secondary schools for blind students. Frustratingly, we don't know if she climbed a pyramid, but she did spend a night "under the shadow of the pyramids." The beauty captivated her. She described it as "a poem . . . I could feel the silence of the desert, intense, primal, hostile to all growth, extending over the noiseless sand in every direction."[18]

Keller's visit thrilled U.S. embassy personnel. The press attention, crowds, fan mail, and the overwhelming number of invitations to speak were "astonishing." The public affairs officer of the U.S. embassy in Egypt reported to the State Department that "so poignant and so universal was her appeal that Miss Keller received by far the widest press coverage of any recent American visitor to Egypt. Miss Keller was described always favorable, often superlatively. . . . The over-all impact of the visit can safely be rated very good to excellent." In bureaucratic language, "all objectives seem to have been successfully attained." Only two months later, Gamal Abdel Nasser would overthrow Egyptian King Farouk. The CIA apparently knew this was coming, but the embassy and the State Department did not. The State Department considered Keller an effective tool to generate positive sentiments toward the United States. This was important as it sought to prevent Egypt from either a policy of neutrality, which the United States interpreted as pro-Soviet sympathies, or allying itself with the Soviet Union.[19]

The initial plan in Damascus, Syria, as it was nearly everywhere, was for Keller to visit associations and schools for blind people. In Damascus, however, there weren't any. Embassy personnel arranged with women prominent in local social welfare efforts to host her. As a result, she visited with members of the Arab Women's Federation and reported with pleasure that Syrian women were "moving rapidly towards social maturity and independence." She praised the women's group, expressing confidence that they would soon start a school for blind people. She also visited a Milk Distribution Center, sponsored by women's social welfare groups, and spoke to the almost 500 women regarding the need for women to actively resolve social problems.[20]

Keller gave another major public lecture in Syria to nearly 700 people, with an additional 200 unable to enter. She reported to Henney, with a bit of pride, that she gave the crowd "the devil because their blind had been utterly neglected." Press reports, however, were universally positive. An embassy staffer reported with delight that twenty-three daily newspapers, five weeklies, and one monthly magazine covered the visit, devoting 1,792 inches to the visit. (Didn't this person have anything else to do?) Newspapers praised her in effusive terms, referring to her as a "miracle" who had "overcome" blindness and deafness. When asked a question about the Arab-Israeli situation, Polly Thomson answered for her and stated that her primary interest was blindness. Embassy personnel declared them "outstanding envoys for the United States."[21]

Embassy personnel reported the same in Jordan. There, as in every country on this trip, she spoke with leading government officials. In this case, the minister of health and social welfare, representatives of the palace, the deputy prime minister, cabinet ministers, and members of the diplomatic corps. The U.S. embassy assessed her contact with the government elite as "most valuable in winning good will for the United States."[22]

Similarly, embassy personnel in Arab Jerusalem reported political pleasure with Helen's visit. The vice consulate wrote that she had avoided political discussion and was received with enthusiasm. Again, newspapers referred to her as the "Miracle of the Twentieth Century." She may not have mentioned politics, but embassy personnel credited her visit with positive political consequence for the United States: "She is one visiting American the Palestinians have accepted wholeheartedly for what she is and about whom no ill is thought and to whom no ulterior motives have been ascribed." Her disability and her miracle status, perhaps her gender, and certainly her willingness to avoid explicit mention of politics, rendered her a powerful political propagandizing tool. Eased by this enthusiasm, local papers made no mention of her subsequent crossing of the military lines into Israel.[23]

Work in Israel on behalf of blind people largely pleased Keller. She wrote to Henney that "the work for the blind and the deaf in Israel has not been exaggerated. . . . Their imagination and resourcefulness help the pupils to overcome lack of equipment and of apparatus that bypass their limitations." Israel's Village of the Blind captivated her. There an entire village of blind people lived in economic self-sufficiency. She criticized the segregation of the group, but residents replied gently that the village served their needs very well. The Israeli nation and government also impressed her. She found it so wonderful, in fact, that "doubters will hardly believe our report." She worried about its future security. Her faith in its present state, however, was reinforced by visits with David Ben Gurion, whom she called "a titan in courage and vision," and Golda Meyerson, who would later become Golda Meier and the Israeli prime minister.[24]

Keller's characterization of Israel differed from other Arab countries. It was an "electric, stimulating atmosphere . . . so different from the putrescent decay of civilizations not yet buried." To Henney, she criticized other Arab countries. The wide disparities of wealth disturbed her, and she wrote of turning "sick at the inconceivable misery and helpless animality" in which refugees lived. She characterized Arabs as having "little sense of social responsibility, and must be pounded and pounded before they adopt an attitude of helpfulness towards the unfortunate."[25]

While Keller did not speak about politics publicly, again she did so to Henney. She addressed U.S. foreign policy rather than the controversial creation of Israel, about which the two had disagreed earlier. She disliked President Truman, but the cold war strategies of his Four-Point Program pleased her. This program provided technological skills, knowledge, and equipment to poor nations throughout the world in order to encourage support of the United States from nations uncommitted in the cold war. She characterized the U.S. delegates working on the program as "heart-warming. . . . Despite the tragic blunderings of America in its foreign policy, just to hear and look at those young men and women absorbed in their global endeavor was a revelation to me of the growing intelligence and spirit of service to others that will yet establish Civilization for all peoples."[26]

State Department records leave little doubt that the government considered Keller an effective propagandizing tool on behalf of the United States. In the postwar and early cold war period, she fostered an image that resonated profoundly on the international stage. The State Department, the U.S. Information Agency, and director Nancy Hamilton's film, *The Unconquered*, contributed to the creation of this image. The international audience saw her as a courageous, interesting, vibrant but quirky old woman (by 1950, she was seventy years old), who had not only endured but also had conquered blindness, deafness, and the vagaries of life that affect all. She represented the United States as a courageous, interesting, vibrant but quirky country that could accomplish virtually anything. The political implications of her actions were implicit, her political opinions left private. Her message was inherently political, but her image was of a living miracle. This seemingly placed her above the squalor of international and partisan politics.

The AFB's involvement with the State Department was not unique. It was not one of the largest private philanthropic organizations in the United States, nor was it involved in high-level discussions. It was one of many philanthropic organizations involved in U.S. diplomacy in the height of the cold war years. Keller's involvement with the State Department was also not unique. She was one of many cultural figures, others were jazz musicians and writers, who joined with the U.S. Information Agency (USIA) to spread U.S. culture.[27]

Keller left little record of how much she knew about and what she thought about her involvement with the State Department. Her support of the Four Point Program, however, is evidence of her enthusiasm for the spread of Americanism during the cold war. She may have been a one-time member of the Socialist Party, but she was also a cold war liberal in support of the spread of Americanism and a woman who found her identity and purpose in international travel.

After leaving Israel in late May 1952, Helen and Polly visited France and Florence Davidson for the first time since Jo's death and joined in the Paris celebrations of the one-hundredth anniversary of Louis Braille's invention of Braille. Nella unsympathetically characterized their midsummer return to the United States as "melancholy . . . partly caused by the letdown from having been treated like princesses when they were abroad," but noted that the heavy schedule of speeches and letters that awaited them had "to a large extent dissipated" their melancholy. Still, she thought them lonely. Nella continued to worry greatly about Polly's health and the lack of an "understudy" in case of Polly's death. As Helen made plans for a South American trip and then a trip to India, Nella complained that "she has no realization that Polly's life may be in danger and [I] must get this unpleasant fact across to her."[28]

Helen clearly did not want to deal with the personal issues of life in the United States. She dove immediately into concerns about Joseph McCarthy and the spreading accusations of communism. She and Robert Duffus, a Westport neighbor and associate editor at the *New York Times*, shared disappointment that President Eisenhower had failed to denounce McCarthy. She praised the *New York Times* August editorial against McCarthy and the paper subsequently published her letter supporting its stand. McCarthy attacked many for reasons far less significant than he could have claimed for Helen, but he did not attack her. Those who looked, including the FBI and the AFB, easily found statements of her progressive political interests that in others would have been highly suspect. The AFB clearly worried about her public political statements. She delighted in having to curb her tongue and in failing to curb her tongue. The admiration of the international and national public ensured her legal safety and public reputation, but it remained grounded in an understanding of her as eternally overcoming inherent deficiencies. This public persona not only kept her from suffering significantly in the witch-hunts of McCarthyism, but also kept her from the public political participation she desired and confined her to issues pertaining to blindness.[29]

Nella Henney understood well Keller's double-edged public persona and tried to shape it. That same fall of 1952, she wrote of Nancy Hamilton's plans for a party celebrating the life and work of Helen Keller (and conveniently timed immediately before the release of Hamilton's 1953 film on Keller, *The Unconquered*, which would ultimately win a 1955 Academy Award[30]). Hamilton hoped to gather a multitude of political and entertainment celebrities, such as Adlai Stevenson, Dwight Eisenhower, Arthur Godfrey, Cardinal Spellman, Eleanor Roosevelt, Marion Anderson, and Bernard Baruch. The intention was to gather people "as far apart in station and belief as possible to give visible evidence that Helen Keller brings all sorts and conditions of men together, their differences forgotten." Henney liked the idea but felt "the premise is false. *It is only when Helen speaks of the blind or the deaf that she brings all mankind together. Politically (and she'll have her say politically or bust) she does not*" [italics added]. Keller's disability grounded her fame and public personhood. When she moved beyond claiming disability as her sole identity, her fame and public efficacy weakened. Those who relied on her for fund-raising knew this. As Henney put it, "She keeps the reactionaries among the AFB trustees on tetherhooks. And Mr. Migel. And Westbrook Pegler and his like." Keller had learned this lesson well by the mid-1920s and repeatedly relearned the lesson in painful ways for the rest of her life.[31]

Henney fiercely policed public film, theatrical, and print representations of Keller but approved of Nancy Hamilton's efforts. In 1950, she, Keller, and AFB staff members had met privately with film director Robert Flaherty about doing a Keller film.[32] The AFB and Henney drove this effort, not the seventy-year-old Keller. Henney expressed "outrage" at Flaherty's "betrayal," after he notified the press about the picture and made it known that he planned to approach Katharine Cornell to appear in the film. He was involved no further. Henney held greater control over Hamilton. She and Keller had first met the director in 1939, when introduced by actress Cornell. Henney and the AFB began film negotiations with Hamilton in 1952, strictly monitoring the production and anything to do with it.[33] The remaining evidence indicates that Keller paid little attention to the film. Henney critiqued the music, the staging, the portrayal of religion in Keller's life, and other details both large and small. She also expressed concern that scenes of the three women in the Keller household (Helen, Anne, and Polly) would fan the already-existing speculation that they were lesbians (or in her words, cause question about whether they were "normal" women).[34]

The resulting film, released as *The Unconquered* in 1953, presents Keller as a charming, slightly quirky, kindly woman, who garners international love and devotion because of her endless and selfless energies. Her disability is overcome; she is unconquered by it; and it serves as the well-spring of her commitment to others. Her politics are sincere but never divisive. This public persona pleased Henney immensely, and she believed it honored Anne Macy appropriately.

In contrast to *The Unconquered*, Nicholas Monsorrat's 1952 book *The Story of Esther Costello* made Henney and the AFB furious. In this story, a deaf-blind young girl, Esther, is rescued from poverty in Ireland by a wealthy American woman Mrs. Manisty. Esther becomes a celebrity and fund-raiser for deaf-blind people, after being taught finger-spelling, but then her fame and its resulting money are exploited ruthlessly by her rescuers. Mr. Manisty rapes her, and the shock then restores her sight and hearing. Henney and the AFB feared this a slur on the memories of John and Anne Macy and an inference that Keller's handlers exploited her for money. Attempting to halt publication of the book, Henney and the AFB wrote letters, threatened lawsuits, and used any influence they could sway. Their only satisfaction was that the book was ultimately a literary failure.[35]

Keller focused her attention not on the film or the book, but on her upcoming 1953 trip to South America and her efforts to finish her book on Anne Macy. Throughout May and June, she visited Brazil, Chile, Peru, Panama, and Mexico. Again, her schedule was frenzied. Secretary of State

John Dulles told diplomatic officers to assist with trip arrangements, and State Department and embassy officials had nothing but praise for her visit. The public affairs officer in Sao Paulo, Brazil, wrote that the publicity she generated exceeded in both quality and quantity that given the previous year's visit of Secretary of State Dean Acheson. Embassy personnel in Lima, Peru, reported that "no private individual" had received as much press attention as Keller in the last year, and that the favorable press would benefit the United States. From Mexico, embassy personnel reported similarly that "no other visitor of any nationality has attracted as much attention from the press or as much public recognition in Mexico during the past several years." The positive press reports she received in "the anti-American, Communist organ *El Popular*" were those most noted by embassy personnel.[36]

Upon returning home, Helen and Polly again exasperated Nella with their restlessness and their plans for yet another international sojourn to India and Japan.

> They both love Arcan Ridge, but they welcome excuses to get away from it. One reason is that they love traveling better than almost anything, the other is that they escape the importunities of correspondence. They are both eager to sit down and talk out the plans for the Teacher book—but they both want to go to India and I am sure will put pressure on the AFOB to send them there. I am also sure that Eric and Robert will oppose it, but the girls may win out. They have before now.[37]

Polly's physical ailments were becoming more visible. The possibility of a stroke haunted Nella and AFB officials. At the same time, home remained a place of unease for Helen. The anti-Communist hysteria of the United States, the continued dissatisfaction and constant turnover of household help, and the loss of many of those she loved pushed her to international venues.

With positive press abroad, and with Keller in her seventies, Henney and others paid increasing attention to how she would be remembered. In early

1952, Henney and the AFB's publicity director began to explore the possibility of nominating Keller for the 1954 Nobel Peace Prize. By the time Helen and Polly returned from South America in 1953, efforts were in earnest. The AFB coordinated the campaign and instructed others—eventually a long list of international supporters—on how to submit and support nominations. AFOB Director Eric Boulter's primary concern was that because George C. Marshall had received the previous award, the Nobel committee would be reluctant to select a U.S. citizen twice in a row.[38] The Nobel Prize effort emphasized Keller's always vague but pleasant-sounding internationalism and transnational efforts to advance the interests of people who were blind. In the words of one nomination letter:

> There will be no need to put special emphasis on Miss Helen Keller's contributions to international peace and good understanding between races through her untiring efforts and services for the blind and other physically handicapped people in the world. It is universally understood that the existence of Miss Keller itself is the most valuable stimulus for those disabled persons, because they can find in her "Victory over the Darkened Silence" a living monument of the possibility of education and human endeavor.

This massive effort included securing endorsements from U.S. congressional members, a failed attempt to convince Secretary of State John Foster Dulles to sign on, and letters of nomination from government officials of at least twelve countries, forty national nongovernmental organizations, and four international nongovernmental organizations. Like the earlier mentioned efforts, this attempted to memorialize Keller as an apolitical woman, who was loved internationally for her cheery countenance in the face of adversity.[39]

Motivated perhaps by the constant assessments of her life, and perhaps aware of her own age, Keller focused on completing the nearly thirty-year effort to write her book on Anne Macy. Nella thought the forced reflection drained Helen emotionally. She asked Nella, "How can I bear the burden of

Formal portrait of Keller in 1955. *Courtesy of the American Foundation for the Blind.*
Used with permission of the American Foundation for the Blind, Helen Keller Archives.

this sacrifice?" and cried over all Anne had given her. Nella helped with editing and thought *Teacher* (1955) a true accomplishment.[40]

Throughout this, Keller, the AFB, and the State Department continued plans for an early 1955 trip to India, Pakistan, Burma, the Philippines, and Japan. Only two months before their departure, Polly mentioned to Nella that it might be their last trip. She was sixty-nine and Helen seventy-four. As Nella recorded the conversation in her diary, "I cut her off, for as long as they are able to travel they will be going forth like this. Then Polly admitted that she thought they could do a great deal more of good in Red China and confessed that she wanted to go to Russia. Helen is no longer starry-eyed about Russia, but she would go."[41]

The AFB, Nella, and others used Helen's departure to stage a Helen Keller love fest, always noting that she would return only days before her seventy-fifth birthday. Harvard bestowed her an honorary degree. The AFB kicked off the trip with a February 1 farewell banquet for 400 at the Waldorf Astoria Hotel in New York City. The U.S. ambassadors from each of the countries she was to visit spoke briefly, followed by Eleanor Roosevelt. Roosevelt spoke effusively of Helen, calling her a "good will ambassador to the world." The photo taken of Keller and Roosevelt appeared in several hundred papers around the world, and eventually won a United Press prize for Bill Sauro. Keller, as always, spoke humbly: "I believe that I am just one of the numberless instruments in God's Hand carrying out His Plan of Good. . . . I only fulfill my mission with both good intent and good effect in helping to eliminate blindness and deafness from the earth, my heart will sing with joy that is Heaven indeed."[42]

The *New York Times* used the occasion of Helen's departure to devote an editorial to her entitled "Courage." The paper noted her age, her upcoming trip, and her "love of democracy and of freedom." She has "a quality of courage," it emphasized, "that enables a few gifted and benign souls to overcome their own handicaps and to give themselves to humanity and for humanity." The press may have helped the trip, but Keller again remained mired in and benefiting from the role of the perpetual *overcomer*. The majority of the public considered disability a personal problem best tackled

Eleanor Roosevelt and Helen Keller at the February 1, 1955, farewell banquet for Keller before her departure for India, Hong Kong, Philippines, and Japan. *Photograph by William Sauro. © Bettmann/CORBIS. Used with permission.*

by, what *Readers' Digest* editors called Keller's "triumph of will and courage." Historian Joanne Meyerowitz argues that editors particularly emphasized the *overcoming* motif in Keller's case to use her as an example of how all women could "overcome seemingly insurmountable barriers."[43]

As in Keller's other travels, the State Department continued its involvement. The AFB added Burma to the itinerary at the request of the State Department, which was apparently concerned by pro-Communist and anti-American sentiments in that country. Embassy personnel characterized her week-long visit as having "an enormous psychological impact favorable to the United States." She berated the Burmese government for its lack of support for blind and deaf citizens. Embassy personnel noted that these comments from anyone else would have generated "grievous resentment," but had prompted action and support when stated by Keller.[44]

India made the largest impression on her. She made her usual visits to schools for blind children, laid the cornerstone for the first workshop for blind adults, and made the rounds of receptions and government officials. Prime Minister Jawaharlal Nehru, claiming the difficult policy of neutrality between the Soviet Union and the United States, charmed her. For pages and pages, she did nothing but praise him to Henney, calling him the "most electrifying expression of India we met." She joined him and his daughter Indira, who would eventually be prime minister herself, for dinner at their home, where they spoke of poetry, philosophy, and economic development.[45]

While the two traveled, Henney, the AFB, and Nancy Hamilton signed contracts with the Motion Picture Division of the USIA. Nella wrote to Helen, ""Nancy has been in touch with the State Department about THE UNCONQUERED and big things may be brewing." Once negotiated, the USIA included *The Unconquered* in its large library of offerings to foreign countries. The USIA program was part of the larger cold war effort to spread Americanism, the message of U.S. goodwill, and propaganda about the positive aspects of U.S. affluence. A partial list of initial film showings includes Manila, Japan, Belgium, Sweden, Germany, the Netherlands, Australia, South Africa, France, Greece, and India. When Keller traveled abroad again, the State Department and the AFB encouraged foreign nations, almost always successfully, to link her visits with viewings of the film.[46]

Helen and Polly never made the threatened trip to the Soviet Union. Both grew increasingly tired, although life at home was never as satisfying as traveling. In 1956, the pair took a personal trip through western Europe, spending most of their time with Polly's family in Scotland. In the spring of 1957, they made their last trip in cooperation with the AFB and the State Department, to Canada, Iceland, Switzerland, Finland, Sweden, Norway, and Denmark. *The Unconquered* was shown everywhere. In Norway, the two addressed a crowd of 10,000 after a lengthy parade. Helen wrote that they "felt like a pair of bloody fools."[47]

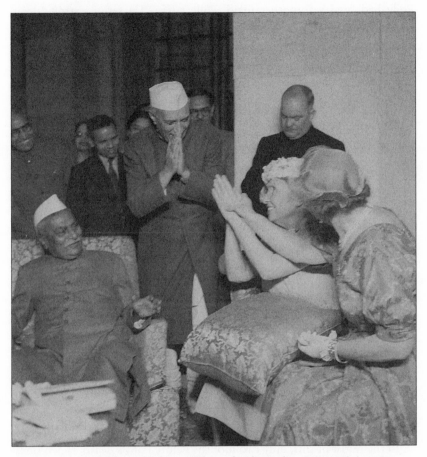

Dr. Rajendra Prasad (seated left), president of India, Indian Prime Minister Jawaharlal Nehru (standing), Helen Keller, and Polly Thomson in New Delhi, India, 1955. *Photograph by Balder Kapoor. © Bettmann/CORBIS. Used with permission.*

Upon returning home, Polly and Helen faced similar but more serious frustrations and complication with their domestic affairs. Travel allowed them to temporarily escape troubles at home but had not made them disappear. Throughout 1957 and 1958, Nella, Nancy Hamilton, Katharine Cornell, and Helen's Harvard friend Lenore Smith grew increasingly concerned about the daily work of maintaining the household at Arcan Ridge.

Polly had fired yet another maid. Polly suffered a serious stroke, from which she never fully recovered, yet she refused to tolerate anyone else finger-spelling to Helen in her presence. Helen required a foot operation. She appeared to care little about the 1962 release of the movie *The Miracle Worker*.

Nella's journals and letters leave clear evidence that throughout the late 1950s and early 1960s, she and others shared increasing concern about who was going to direct Keller's affairs and money. Since 1932, trustees of the Helen Keller Trust Fund had managed her financial affairs. By this period, most of Helen's friends had died, the initial trustees were having to be replaced, and those friends that remained sometimes acrimoniously debated control of her affairs. Though there is no evidence of fiduciary wrongdoing, Nella feared the possibility. She may also have been angry that she wasn't selected as a trustee. She repeatedly wrote of being awakened by "bad dreams" about Helen and her future.[48]

Throughout 1959, Polly's health grew worse and she died in March 1960. Helen attended funeral services in Bridgeport, Connecticut, but balked when her trustees arranged for the urn containing Polly's ashes to be deposited at the National Cathedral next to those of Anne Macy. She did not want the ashes there and refused to attend the committal. Polly mattered, but what mattered most was the personal and historical linkage between the teacher Anne Sullivan Macy and the student Helen Keller.

In the midst of this, only two months before Polly's death, Helen unexpectedly and without explanation broke off her relationship with Nella. The reasons are unclear. Nella blamed it on Polly's growing attitude of possessiveness toward Helen and her consequent efforts to eliminate other influences in Helen's life. Keller biographer Joseph Lash contends that Helen may have grown to believe Nella was exploiting her financially and thus terminated the relationship. Dorothy Herrmann, author of the most recent biography, believes Helen may have grown increasingly frustrated with her "keepers" and their tendency to present her as a modern day saint. Nella was the keeper most easily dismissed, and so she was. In September 1961, Helen reestablished contact with Nella, but the relationship was never as smooth. Helen lost her most steadfast companion of the previous thirty-four years when she rejected Nella. Few people remained in her life. No one remained who was as steadfastly committed to her intellectual stimulation, constantly sending or arranging to send Braille versions of news and literature, as Nella had been.[49]

Through and after the years of Polly's illness, Winifred Corbally and Evelyn Seide, two women who had helped at Arcan Ridge and knew finger-spelling, continued to assist Helen with daily activities. Corbally remembered the years with fondness: "Those were the fun years. It was a time of her life when she could have fun. Miss Helen was a rogue. . . . We had oodles of fun. We would go to a hot-dog stand. Polly Thomson would turn in her grave. She would never allow hot dogs in the house. But Miss Helen loved them. 'Don't forget the mustard,' she would say."

In October 1961, Helen suffered her first stroke and retired from public life. Over the next seven years, she experienced numerous other strokes, difficulties with diabetes, and largely lived in her wheelchair and bed.

In 1964, President Lyndon Johnson honored her with the Presidential Medal of Freedom.

In 1968, Helen Keller died at eighty-eight years of age.[50]

5

One of the Least
Free People on Earth

The Making and Remaking of Helen Keller

Helen wants to be free and tries to be but is actually one of
the least free people on earth.
—Nella Braddy Henney, 1947

In Helen Keller's birthplace of Tuscumbia, Alabama, tourists can purchase
Helen Keller throw blankets, Helen Keller silver spoons, Helen Keller key
chains, Helen Keller magnets, Helen Keller coffee cups, Helen Keller water
jugs, two different Helen Keller t-shirts, a first-day issue of the postal
stamp featuring Keller and her teacher Anne Sullivan, three-inch replicas
of *the* water pump, and because Alabama summers are hot, several Helen
Keller paper fans. During the yearly Helen Keller Festival, one can earn a
ribbon in the Helen Keller 5K-run or view the Helen Keller parade. One can
visit the Helen Keller Hospital, the Helen Keller Public Library, the Helen
Keller tennis courts, or walk through the Helen Keller car show. Tourists
can also view a production of *The Miracle Worker* at the Keller home. Those
with cash remaining can purchase many of the over 200 books currently in
print, most of them for children, about Helen Keller. The public memory
of Helen Keller is, it seems, a veritable industry—not only in Tuscumbia,
Alabama, but everywhere.[1]

Today's memorials to Helen Keller—films, her grave site, statutes, small
town festivals, books, the millions of elementary schools bearing her
name, and the 2003 Alabama quarter—continue to shape our public

memories of her. In powerful but subtle ways, they reflect and create contemporary social understandings of disability, gender, and the public body.
Virtually, all emphasize her fame and effectiveness as a symbol and seek to
sustain that symbol. They also reflect competing efforts to create the Keller
legacy and the two predominant images that have emerged in popular culture: the young and virginal deaf-blind girl overcoming great personal
tragedy; and the peace-loving international figure adored unquestioningly
by all citizens of the globe.

Considerable effort went into shaping our shared public memories of
Keller long before she died in 1968. Initially, some of those around her
sought to keep her controversial politics out of the public eye, or sought to
eliminate them altogether, in the belief that such politics would make
fund-raising difficult. In the later years of her life, those around her sought
to shape a public memory of an inspirational internationalist with vague
politics. Though no one openly said they expected her to die soon, the AFB
and particularly Nella Braddy Henney began *explicit* legacy-building efforts
in 1950. For example, Henney policed the proposed film by Robert Flaherty as well as Nancy Hamilton's *The Unconquered*. She and the AFB also
played a pivotal role in the nomination of Keller for the 1954 Nobel Peace
Prize.

Beyond films and Nobel Prizes, Henney and sometimes Doubleday editor Ken McCormick (her initial employer and Keller's longtime publisher)
strictly monitored and attempted to control anything published about or
even daring to mention Keller. In 1954, Henney expressed indignation that
Grace Murphy, a virtually unknown deaf woman, mentioned Keller, very
benignly, in her memoir on her own deafness. Henney managed to insult
deaf people, in general, in the process: "I find Mrs. Murphy rather appalling—insensitive and aggressive and I think she would have been without the deafness." That same fall she worried about the inclusion of a picture of Keller in a book on the 1912 Lawrence strike: "The book is obvi-
ously propaganda—very skillfully done—and we need to know more about
the political complexion of those behind it."[2] In the next few years, other
books appeared that were directly, indirectly, or just possibly about Keller.

These caused Henney great concern. In September 1957, she wrote in her diary, "Toward the end of a miserable summer. Helen's eczema gets better, gets worse. . . . Meanwhile the worries continue: the Tibble book, the book by Mrs. Roosevelt's friend (Miss or Mrs. Hickock)[Lorena Hickock], the impending release of the Esther Costello picture, etc. And so it will ever be as long as Helen lives."[3]

In 1956, Henney acknowledged to McCormick that they could not "prevent other people from writing about Helen" but suggested that they "control the source material." Doubleday held copyright on virtually everything Keller had published. In 1957 and 1958, they began to plan the timing of what she called the "Helen Keller Omnibus." McCormick reassured her that this was not "ghoulish preparation" on their part.[4] He presumably remained on his toes. Earlier Henney had warned him that "if through carelessness or for any other avoidable reason anything develops at Doubleday's or elsewhere that I feel is injurious to Helen I intend to raise all the hell I can with all the help I can get."[5]

The influence of Henney and the AFB over the cultural memories of Keller continued even after her 1968 death—and even after Henney's death in 1973. The AFB purposefully began to collect archival materials by 1971. Author Ralph G. Martin, who had written on Keller in 1962, sought access to the AFB's materials to write a biography, but Robert Barnett of the AFB assured Henney that Martin would not be allowed to see her material without permission. She disliked him, claiming his previous publications were "gossip books." She warned the AFB that "Helen's image is bright and beautiful all over this world and I would fight like everything to keep it from being tarnished."[6] After Henney died, her husband Keith monitored Keller biographies. He apparently approved of Joseph Lash as Keller's biographer. Lash's qualifications were unquestionable: he had won the Pulitzer Prize for his biography of Franklin and Eleanor Roosevelt, had met Keller, knew some of her social circle, and held similar political views. Marguerite Levine, librarian at the AFB, assured Mr. Henney that Lash was appropriate: "Working with Mr. Lash is a joy. His opus will be a tribute not only to Helen but also to Nella who was the lifeline keeping her in touch with the world. For all her devotion Polly would never have been able to interpret the political, literary and scientific events of the world which Helen found so stimulating."[7]

Henney not only cared about shaping our historical memories of Keller but also succeeded in doing so through her own vast collection of letters and journals. No one else, not even Keller, the AFB, and certainly not Anne Macy, left such a rich and accessible collection. Henney was determined that Keller be remembered as an inspirational and international figure of caring, the miraculous product of the highly skilled Anne Sullivan Macy. She devoted decades of her life to maintaining a rich intellectual and social circle for Keller, perhaps partially to fulfill a commitment to Anne Macy. By leaving this considerable collection of historical materials, Henney also guaranteed that her voice continues to be heard and her influence continues to hold sway—perhaps even to the exclusion of others.

What is Helen Keller's favorite color?
Corduroy.

How did Helen Keller's parents punish her?
They rearranged the furniture.

One of the primary means by which popular culture maintains our shared memory of Helen Keller is through her own genre of jokes. What does the continued success and circulation of Helen Keller jokes tell us? Behind closed doors, and without academic lenses, they may be funny. Scholars may try to be serious about their work and may tend to be pretentious, but an "analysis" of a thick file of Keller jokes produces smiles. Perhaps the jokes tell us less about Keller and more about the continued strength of her legacy and dominant cultural attitudes regarding disability.

Folklorist Mac E. Barrick writes that while Helen Keller jokes circulated in the late 1960s and early 1970s, their popularity skyrocketed after a 1979 NBC television presentation of *The Miracle Worker*. He traces some of the Keller jokes directly to play and film productions of *The Miracle Worker*. For example, the "moved furniture" jokes relate to the scene in which the newly arrived Miss Sullivan rearranges the furniture of the garden cottage so that young Helen doesn't know where she is. With the new 1979 production, once again the story of the young and radically transformed Helen was common cultural currency. The popularity of Keller jokes occurred simultaneous with the increased integration of children with physical and cognitive disabilities into the public school system, and simultaneous with the success and visibility of the disability rights movement's demands for physical and programmatic access to public facilities. Barrick argues that jokes about children with physical and cognitive disabilities grew also. These concurrent events most likely contributed to the popularity of the Keller joke. Mention Helen Keller and the joking public instantaneously understand her to represent all those who are sightless, all those who use a tactile language, and perhaps even all people with disabilities. Keller was and is the most easily recognizable and acceptable public figure for *any* form of disability humor.[8]

Scholar James Loewen points out that the Keller jokes may be an attempt to deal with the sanitized, "goody-goody" version of the woman that dominates our cultural memories. With these jokes, children deflate "a pretentious symbol that is too good to be real." Mary Klages suggests that this may be a gendered process. Girls are much more likely to read about, perhaps admire, and perhaps be compared to Helen Keller. Girls also tend to be more aware of social propriety and politeness, often considered a "feminine" responsibility. Thus, girls might tell fewer Keller jokes, ever mindful of propriety; on the other hand, girls might tell more Keller jokes, transgressing oppressive behavioral prescriptions and denying Keller's supposedly ideal politeness, asexuality, and demure nature.[9]

To "get" a Helen Keller joke one must know who Helen Keller is and what she represents: a deaf-blind heroine remembered for overcoming her seemingly horrendous disability in a cheerful and heroic fashion. As Klages points out, "the key to understanding and responding to Helen Keller jokes lies in knowing on some level what the dominant cultural representations of Keller point out as the moral lesson her life teaches—that handicaps are things to be overcome." Her uniqueness as the dominant cultural figure of U.S. disability, and the character of our cultural memories of her, make the jokes possible.[10]

Tasteless jokes are not new or unique to the Helen Keller genre. Speaking the inappropriate is part of the excitement and humor of many joke genres, including the raunchy joke. The polio outbreaks of the 1950s and the thalidomide scare of the 1960s generated their own string of jokes. Racist, sexist, disability, gay and lesbian jokes weave a continuous and intersecting thread throughout U.S. history. Example: Q: Why couldn't Helen Keller drive? A: She was a woman. These jokes reflect and teach attitudes about social groups. They serve to shock. They also allow individuals to express social unease, ranging from discomfort to hate, that would be unacceptable to express in other ways.[11]

In jokes and in conversation, Helen Keller sometimes is used, as a synonym for incompetence and the inability to function, to insult others. For example, when U.S. House Speaker Newt Gingrich wanted to insult special prosecutor Kenneth Starr in 1998, he called him "the Helen Keller of American politics." The incompetent theme also appears in jokes. Example: Q: How did Helen Keller burn her left ear? A: Answering the iron. Q: How did Helen Keller burn her right ear? They called back. This usage of Keller jokes questions the capability of Keller and other people with disabilities to function on a daily basis.[12]

"Getting" a Helen Keller joke also requires knowing that it will meet with social disapproval, otherwise the telling and enjoyment of the joke would not be transgressive. These jokes are considered inappropriate, and thus funny, because "our dominant cultural attitude toward disability is strictly limited to feelings of pity, charity, and sympathy." Every Keller joke teller defies taboos against ridiculing those "less fortunate," and disregards dominant cultural attitudes of patronizing benevolence that consider people with disabilities as childlike, dependent, and in need of protection. In many ways, telling these jokes *is* truly transgressive, because they so clearly claim the bodies, the physicality, the visibility, the differences, and the defiant nature of people with disabilities. At the same time, Keller jokes fail to contradict the cultural attitudes about disability they disregard, because they depend on these very same attitudes for their success.[13]

The sex genre of Helen Keller jokes blends stereotypes about blindness and deafness with pornographic humor to lampoon Keller's virginal and saintly character. Example: Q: Why does Helen Keller masturbate with one hand? A: So she can moan with the other. These jokes depend on cultural attitudes that define people with disabilities as asexual, and cultural attitudes about Helen Keller that consider the possibility of her sexuality as absurd, and then force the listener to confront the possibility of a sexual Helen Keller. She is famous for transcending, overcoming, leaving her body and all its limitations behind. Helen Keller sex jokes force recognition of the bodies, the physicality, and the sexuality of people with disabilities.[14]

Jokes about Keller's sexuality are also funny because our shared cultural memories of her are *not* as a sexual person. In fact, we tend to think of her on the opposite end of the sexual spectrum: as asexual as one can be. She was too young (after all, doesn't her story often end at the pump?), too old, too single, too virginal, too blind, too deaf. Cultural values and stereotypes have conditioned us to interpret all these traits as indicating asexuality.

In fact, Keller lived a very sensual life. Her entire means of communicating with other individuals, of companionship, was tactile. She continually touched other people in very intimate ways and in very intimate moments of their lives. To communicate with her, people touched her in a reciprocal and intimate fashion. Her disability also created occasions for her to touch other people in a manner that was socially unacceptable for virtually anyone but her. For example, she is likely the only one to have slowly, thoroughly, and almost intimately run her fingers around the face of each U.S. president from Cleveland to Kennedy. She also, like many people with disabilities, was often physically and personally isolated from other people. Touch was her only means of contact.

Nella Henney feared that visual images of Keller communicating by touching other women, largely Anne Macy or Polly Thomson, conveyed the impression that she was lesbian. Consequently, she monitored visual images. On at least one occasion when asked about the matter, she carefully assured the inquirers that the women of the Keller household were heterosexual. Others also questioned the heterosexuality and sexual nature of Keller's various relationships. Biographer Joseph Lash recorded, but never included in his biography, the various opinions and speculations of people he interviewed that John Macy had sexual relations with both women when married to Anne, that Anne and Helen were lovers, that Helen had gay friends, and that Polly was lesbian. My research resulted in no evidence of any lesbian relationships; nor did it result in evidence of heterosexual relationships. Very few historical figures leave any proof, outside of bearing children, of their sexual relations. Keller is no different.[15]

What interests me is the discomfort with which so many consider Keller's sexuality. She knew that her intense tactile nature made people uneasy—especially, she noted, *men*. When she spoke with those who did not finger-spell, she sat very close to them. With her left index finger, middle finger, and thumb she touched their nostril, lips, and larynx in order to understood their words. This disconcerted men particularly. "They [men] get embarrassed," she said, "and start to stammer." Keller's touch and constant tactile nature flustered and confused many, particularly those whose only framework by which to understand touch was sexual.[16]

The resulting anxiety is exacerbated by further contradictions. Descriptions of her physicality at almost all ages emphasize her beauty. She learned to charm those around her, and particularly men, easily and successfully. At all ages, she and others took great care that she appear pretty and appealing in a conventionally heterosexual fashion. At the same time, Keller and other women with disabilities often encounter the assumption that they are asexual and that expressing sexuality is inappropriate for them. "Seen as the opposite of the masculine figure, but also imagined as the antithesis of the normal woman, the figure of the disabled female is thus ambiguously positioned both inside and outside the category of woman." Physically attractive, and disabled, to many Keller literally embodies contradiction. This embodied contradiction, however, may have lent to the charges of lesbianism to those who consider any female bodily deviance equivalent to lesbianism.[17]

Part of the unease regarding Keller's sexuality may also be due to her carefully crafted global reputation as a virginal figure. Her primary cultural representations are that of a young deaf-blind girl who overcame tragedy and that of a benevolent international purveyor of goodwill. Neither representation can remain steadfast if it incorporates sexuality or is sullied by passion of any kind. If they had been compelled to consider even the possibility of her sexuality, those around her might well have felt uneasy.

Some may have speculated on Keller's sexuality in order to humanize her. Considering her sexually could, with derision, force the adored heroine off the pedestal. But such consideration could also lovingly reconnect the isolated heroine to other human beings both figuratively and literally. For others, there may have been a hint of voyeurism in the suppositions about Keller's sexuality. They could watch and speculate about her without her being aware. She knew people looked at her without her explicit knowledge, and it made her uneasy. Others may have simply been curious.

Finally, charges of lesbianism or sexual nonconformity are and have been frequently thrown at public women. Gender traditionalists frequently assume that any woman living nontraditional gender roles must also fail to adhere to traditional sexual norms. Opponents of suffragists, feminists, and other female reformers have also often called them lesbians or sexual deviants in order to discredit them and their political ideologies. Fearing the consequences of such accusations, many women have correspondingly curtailed their public activities. The speculations about Keller's sexuality, and the casting of it as abnormal, may simply be another example of this tactic.

Keller sought and worked hard to attain the appearance of physical *normality*, for while her fame lay entirely in the disability of her body, she and others sought to hide it. Beauty and approval meant appearing *not* disabled. Those around her reinforced the view that appearing disabled made her less acceptable. Anne Macy, for example, wrote that when she first saw the child Helen, "I did not mind the tumbled hair, the soiled pinafore, the shoes tied with the strings—all that could be remedied in time, but if she had been deformed, or had acquired any of those nervous habits that so often accompany blindness . . . how much harder it would have been for me!"[18]

Others praised her as nearly perfect physically, except for what was almost always framed as a fatal physical beauty flaw—her disability. At seventeen years of age, a newspaper reporter described her as "a handsome, well-formed, graceful girl. The waist of her dress fits loosely, and there are no suggestions of corsets or of tight bands about the young girls' waist or neck." Her hands, he wrote, "are delights to the eye, and the extraordinary sensitiveness of their finger-tips cannot be imagined by one who has only the usual sense of touch. Her chief beauty, next to her hands, is the mass of short brown hair that falls on her shoulders and which is confined only by a small comb. . . . Her chin is beautifully formed, the mouth and teeth are good, her complexion is clear and healthy and the expression of her face wonderfully attractive in its bright alertness." To this writer, the tragedy was that "looking at the face you are struck first, of course, by the pathos of the eyes that show all too plainly their affliction. Aside from these there is nothing to sadden one in Helen Keller's appearance." The disability elicited sadness and marred her beauty.[19]

With these overwhelming cultural attitudes, it is no surprise that Keller sought to appear nondisabled in photographs and in person.[20] Prior to 1909, because her left eye protruded she only appeared in photographs in profile. In 1909, doctors removed her eyes and replaced them with glass eyes tinted blue. From this point forward, front-facing photographs of her were common. She, household members, and family members kept her glass eyes secret. A reporter in the early 1930s praised her blue eyes, saying they had "none of the lack-luster look usual to the blind. When she talks, they take on animation; and they gaze at you with what seems a seeing glance."[21]

Keller also sought to appear nondisabled in order to avoid being stared at. In *Midstream* (1929) she wrote, "Oh, the weariness of sitting hours upon hours in the same attitude as I have to do sometimes, not daring to look around or move an arm lest I be stared at or my uncertain movements misconstrued! I cannot see people staring at me; but I am always accompanied by persons who can see, and it is embarrassing to them." While she probably remained unaware of when or where a specific person stared at her, she knew it was done. Keller knew that staring, as Rosemarie Garland-Thomson explains it, "gives meaning to impairment by marking it as aberrant." It created a power dynamic that "constitute[d] the starer as normal and the object of the stare as different," even if she was unaware of the specific incidents of staring. In her chronicle for public consumption quoted above, *Midstream*, she insists she avoided stares not for her sake, but for the sake of those who accompanied her. One wonders if this was true. The intense energy she devoted to her public presentation suggests it was not.[22]

Keller and others around her developed and maintained a strong sense of womanly disability propriety: acceptable physicality and behavior for the disabled woman. This included appropriate displays of eyes, hair, clothing, and posture. In this effort she, Macy, and Polly Thomson devoted considerable energy and time. Disability propriety also included behavior. For example, in 1956, Keller characterized finger-spelling to herself an unnecessary physical display of her disability, a severe sin. "Helen sinned in another way by spelling constantly to herself with her fingers, even after she had learned to speak with her mouth." This bothered her such that "I determined to stop spelling to myself before it became a habit I could not break, and so I asked her [Macy] to tie my fingers up in paper. . . . the experiment succeeded except that even now, in moments of excitement, or when I wake from sleep, I occasionally catch myself spelling with my fingers." For someone of the oralist tradition, signing to oneself may have been seen as repulsive behavior and evidence of inferiority.[23]

One of the ironies, of course, of Keller's efforts to appear not disabled is that her fame and public personhood were literally embodied in the disability of her body. Her ability to be *disabled* while appearing nondisabled was what made her famous. Her efforts to appear *normal* made the supposed overcoming of her disability seem all the more miraculous. Her ability to perform "the selfhood, the subjectivity, of a nondisabled person" resulted in the further emphasis of her disability. Additionally, the *normalcy* of appearance that she sought was defined in opposition to the disability that she embodied to so many people. As Lennard Davis argues, "the very concept of normalcy by which most people (by definition) shape their existence is in fact tied inexorably to the concept of disability, or rather, the concept of disability is a function of the concept of normalcy. Normalcy and disability are part of the same system."[24]

Unlike Franklin Roosevelt, she could not hide her disability. As Davis argues, "Roosevelt was determined that people should not define him in this stigmatized role, and he managed the reception of his image so that he would not be, in our terms, a disruption in the visual field." Roosevelt knew that a successful political career required that he not be visibly disabled. With sophistication he and others engineered public images that generally downplayed the extent of his disability, dismissing it as overcome, done with, or of no consequence.[25]

Keller had no such choice. Her disability could not be kept invisible and her public persona depended on the attention paid to it. She lived the daily contradiction of seeking a public presence in a culture in which her femaleness and disability imposed seclusion in the private sphere. Her efforts to build a political and public career rested on the shaky ground of her visible disability, her visible female gender, and her visible radical politics. Whether she intended it or not, being seen, disrupting the visual field, became a radical move.

It is ironic that neither Keller, the AFB, Nella Henney, nor her publisher had direct involvement in developing the most widely embraced Helen Keller memorial from this period: *The Miracle Worker*. This 1957 play penned by William Gibson, and then the 1962 film version directed by Arthur Penn that earned both Patty Duke and Anne Bancroft Oscars, continues to be seen by millions every year. It was remade for television in 1979 with an adult Patty Duke in the role of Sullivan and next remade for television in 2000 by Disney. The content of the play escaped the vigorous supervision of Henney, although she did become intensely involved in the legal negotiations with Gibson. Keller lunched with Anne Bancroft in 1959, but Henney thought her only "mildly interested" in the stage production of *The Miracle Worker*.[26]

The play focuses on Anne Sullivan Macy's initial education of the child Helen, and its title refers to Macy as the worker of miracles. William Gibson ironically noted, after its reception and all the attention paid to Keller, that the play should have been called "The Miracle Workee." Or as writer Georgina Kleege explains the title, Macy "was the one who worked the miracle, and triumphed over adversity. You [Keller] were the adversity she overcame." Henney and others cared most about our public memory of Keller's adulthood but because of *The Miracle Worker*, we remember her primarily as a child. The young Helen of *The Miracle Worker* is an animalistic and uncontrollable child, ruled by her bodily disabilities. Anne Sullivan miraculously transforms the child by forcing her unruly disabled body to obedience and then to language. The play, and now Keller's life, is generally interpreted as a story of civilization and humanity—in the form of language—conquering the disobedient and inhuman disabled body of the young Helen. It measures people with disabilities, in the analysis of Mary Klages, "by their ability to transcend, or not marginalize, their bodily differences."[27]

Today one of the most public physical memorials to Helen Keller is her home in Tuscumbia, Alabama. Tuscumbia is a small town, currently being crowded by urban sprawl, that prides itself as her birthplace. The birthplace and Tuscumbia's yearly *Helen Keller Festival* feed and feed on *The Miracle Worker* memory.

The physical centerpiece of the Tuscumbia festival and the Tuscumbia memorial is the Helen Keller home, Ivy Green. This national historic site is funded, owned, and run by the nonprofit city-based Helen Keller Property Board. One enters from the front drive, the house is straight ahead, the garden cottage where Anne Sullivan and the young Helen were briefly isolated is to the right, and the pump is behind and between the two buildings. The small house is staffed largely by local women. On the main floor is a very small formal museum space that includes lots of pictures of Keller with other famous people and a few historical relics, one labeled "From the War Between the States." The dining room is set with china. At my visit the guide explained that young Helen was born a "normal" child but after her blindness and deafness she became very unmanageable. The china displayed is all that remains because the pre-Sullivan Helen had broken most of it. The site is inaccessible to anyone with a mobility impairment and the only Braille is a book displayed for the examination of the presumed-sighted children who visit. As James Loewen pointed out in *Lies Across America*, in Tuscumbia Keller is presented as a "bland source of optimistic inspiration." Her adult life is rarely scrutinized; and when it is, it is as an apolitical person who just wanted to be nice to others. Festival brochures mark the site as overwhelmingly white.[28]

The emotional centerpiece of the Tuscumbia festival and the Tuscumbia memorial is the live performances of *The Miracle Worker* that take place every weekend all summer long. Behind the Keller house is a permanent stage and seating area of approximately eighty folding chairs and uncomfortable high school-like bleachers. As is usual with this play, members of the audience have difficulty deciding with whom they are supposed to identify. The long dining room scene, in which Keller and Macy violently and messily battle over her mode of eating and table manners, contains no dialogue. Sometimes the audience laughed at the physical struggles and food flying between the pair. The laughter, however, was uncomfortable as few seemingly knew how to respond. Did laughter give the impression that they were ridiculing people with disabilities? Might it seem voyeuristic? Pity seemed even less appropriate. Even if sentimentalized pity was acceptable, however, should it be directed at the young Helen or at Miss Sullivan? Children in the audience had less of a struggle. They delighted in the ways that the child Helen fought the adult Miss Sullivan. She throws food and silverware, pulls hair, bites, and does everything that children, particularly girl children, are not supposed to do.

The story, of course, ends with the climactic moment at the pump. In that moment, Miss Sullivan breaks through the wall of the young Helen's disability. By acquiring language, the child becomes human. Her family re-joices. The story ends. Some of the china will remain intact. Audience members have another opportunity to purchase their three-inch replicas of *the* pump.

One cannot help but wonder what Keller would have thought. This ex-pansive memorial builds on the version of her life that ignores the politics she fought so hard to express and generally ignores the adulthood she grew into. It defines disability as a primitive condition conquered and overcome by the taming influence of education. It is also distinct from the expansive and liberal internationalism that Nella Braddy Henney at-tempted to memorialize that defined disability as, when overcome, the wellspring of human love and generosity. But in addition, it exalts the ped-agogical skills of Anne Macy, about which Keller cared immensely.

Keller left infuriatingly little indication of how she wanted to be re-membered. We do know that she desperately wanted to be interred next to Macy at the National Cathedral, where the two today share a crypt. When Polly Thomson died in 1960, Keller fought against Henney and the AFB to keep from having Thomson interred with them. Maintaining her primary identification with her beloved Teacher, and her teacher with herself, was intensely important to her. She certainly didn't want Thomson intruding on the historical linkage of Anne Sullivan Macy and Helen Keller, teacher and pupil. Maintaining Macy's memory as the ultimate educator was far more important to her than her own memorials.[29]

Keller cared about how she was remembered. Throughout her eighty-eight years, she sought fiercely to shape her own life, actions, and options, frequently defying those around her. She played an active role in the devel-opment and maintenance of a public persona that benefited her greatly. To those who knew her well, she was more interesting and complex than either the child at the well or the benign and well-intended international-ist. Both of these false images deny the social, political, and economic con-sequences for Keller and others of twentieth-century conceptions of dis-ability.

. . .

139

Historians build our stories about the past from historical evidence—letters, diaries, newspaper reports, published materials, photographs, and organizational and government records. In Keller's case the material is circumscribed. Anne Macy burnt her own diary and other personal materials. John Macy left virtually nothing. Keller's home at Arcan Ridge burnt in 1946, and the bulk of what she had was destroyed. Henney tried to find consolation from the fire's shaping of the way history would remember Keller: "The only comfort that she and I could find was that many decisions which we had never felt ourselves qualified to make had been taken from us. Some of these—destruction of letters and papers Teacher herself had not been equal to. We make a new start." The loss of the presumably hundreds or thousands of letters written to Keller by deaf, blind, and deaf-blind people from around the world is colossal. From these we could have learned a great deal about the everyday lives of people with disabilities.[30]

What remains of Keller's personal papers after the 1946 house fire are maintained at the American Foundation for the Blind headquarters in New York. Why they are there is somewhat disputed. Keller sent personal items to the AFB periodically throughout her life, and as material pertaining to her AFB-organized travels accumulated, they remained there. Henney wrote that for most of her adult life Keller planned to will her remaining personal papers to the Library of Congress. At the height of her efforts to shape Keller's legacy, fearing how the AFB might use the materials, Henney made the necessary legal arrangements with the Library of Congress. Around the time of Keller's break with Henney, however, Keller stipulated that everything go to the American Foundation for the Blind. Whether or not this was a new or ongoing desire on her part is not clear. Robert Barnett of the AFB told Keller's biographer, Joseph Lash, that Keller had always wanted her papers to be with the AFB, and that Henney alone had arranged for them to be at the Library of Congress, using her legal power of attorney.[31]

However the historical collection got to the AFB, the result shapes our memories of her. The AFB keeps the materials publicly available, and a new effort is currently underway to improve the guides that help historians find their way through the large collection. Viewing the AFB materials, however, requires much greater initiative on the part of the scholar than would a trip to a public library facility. The material is simply less available than it would be at the Library of Congress.

Finally, the attack on the World Trade Center in September 2001 destroyed some of the material held at the office of Helen Keller International (initially a subsidiary and now a relative of the AFB). As of the latest report, no one is sure what materials were there and whether or not copies exist.[32] Keller's decision to leave her material to the AFB is one of the reasons professionally trained scholars have had little part in the public memorializing of one of the world's most famous women.

How and whether we remember Keller does matter. Her humanity did not begin at the pump in a symbolic baptism. This type of veneration defines disability as a personal tragedy best dealt with by perpetual acts of overcoming. Nor did her life culminate in the blandness of teary-eyed internationalism promoted during and immediately after her lifetime by Henney and the AFB. This defines disability as a personal tragedy that generates either sainthood, as in Keller's case; or possibly, but generally left unstated, degeneracy. Both of these cultural memories mark disability as the exception, the unusual, and the Other. Both mark disability as a private occurrence distinct from the public realm of justice, discrimination, economic consequence, and activism. Both serve to closet the world's most famous out-of-the-closet person with a disability.

Memorializing Keller's international life as one of bland, teary-eyed niceness also characterizes her political activities as inherently apolitical. This defines her activities, opinions, and activism as insignificant and inconsequential; just as it does the activities, opinions, and activism of many other women. It also encourages overlooking the historical incidence, depth, and breadth of U.S. radicalism.

In his analysis of historical heroes, James Loewen argues: "We seem to feel that a person like Helen Keller can be an inspiration only so long as she remains uncontroversial, one-dimensional. We don't want complicated icons." We now understand the effort it took, by many people, to flatten

Keller's profile. Memorializing her by sanitizing her to the point of blandness is historically false, just as it binds our contemporary understandings of disability, U.S. radicalism, and women's political activities. Keller is a complicated icon, just as she was a complicated individual, who lived a complicated life. She thrived, however, on complication, on debate, on excitement, and on constant movement. She liked Scotch, not tea.[33]

Notes

Abbreviations: HK (Helen Keller), PT (Polly Thomson), NBH (Nella Braddy Henney), Migel (M. C. Migel).

NOTES TO THE INTRODUCTION

1. Foner, *Helen Keller*.
2. Keller, "If You Have Friends You Can Endure Anything," *American Magazine*, September 1929, 62. For an account of this meeting, see Lash, *Helen and Teacher*, 48.
3. Baynton, *Forbidden Signs*, 55.
4. Keller, "If You Have Friends You Can Endure Anything," 63.
5. Small "d" deaf refers to people who are deaf. Capital "D" Deaf refers to people who are deaf culturally; that is, they are part of and identify with Deaf culture. For further information on the Deaf community in the twentieth century, see Burch, *Signs of Resistance*.
6. Keller, *Story of My Life*, 32.
7. Keller describes meeting Bridgman in *Midstream*, 245–247. Freeberg, *The Education of Laura Bridgman*; Gitter, *The Imprisoned Guest*.
8. Howe had met Brace before he met Bridgman but considered her, at eighteen, too old to learn. Wait, "Julia Brace"; Waterhouse, "Education of the Deaf-Blind in the United States of America, 1837–1967"; Lane, *When the Mind Hears*, 255–260.
9. Herrmann, *Helen Keller*, 40, 60–61.
10. Keller, *The Story of My Life*, 44.
11. Keller, *Midstream*, 75.
12. Brooks, *Helen Keller*, 87.
13. Einhorn, *Helen Keller*, 80.
14. Kudlick, "The Outlook of *The Problem* and the Problem with the *Outlook*."
15. For further analysis of "overcoming," see Linton, *Claiming Disability*, 17–19.
16. Finger, "Helen and Frida," 403. For further insights into Franklin Delano Roosevelt, see Gallagher, *FDR's Splendid Deception*.
17. This field and my discussion of it rely on a growing array of academic research. For a beginning sampling, see Thomson, *Extraordinary Bodies*; Davis, *Bending*

over Backwards, especially chapter 2; Longmore and Umansky, *The New Disability History*; Linton, *Claiming Disability*; Davis, *The Disability Studies Reader*; Mitchell and Snyder, *The Body and Physical Difference*.

NOTES TO CHAPTER 1

1. Keller, *Teacher*, 37.

2. Baynton, "Disability and the Justification of Inequality in American History."

3. Keller, *The Story of My Life*, 44. Keller dealt with both of these arguments in "An Apology for Going to College," in *Out of the Dark*, 83–106. Herrmann, *Helen Keller*, 115–118; Lash, *Helen and Teacher*, 217–220, 263.

4. Keller, *Teacher*, 97; Keller, *The Story of My Life*, 50.

5. Lash, *Helen and Teacher*, 262; Keller, *Midstream*, 10; Keller, *The Story of My Life*, 53, 63.

6. Keller, *Midstream*, 15

7. Ibid., 6; Lash, *Helen and Teacher*, 282, 323–324; Herrmann, 140–143.

8. Keller, *Midstream*, 23. Lenore Smith sometimes went with Keller to course lectures in order to finger-spell them to her when Sullivan was unable to do so. Keller, *Midstream*, 20.

9. Ibid., 13. Keller made a similar but abbreviated claim in 1913. When asked if she would rather have sight and hearing, but lack the intellect she had to understand the world, she quickly replied that she would rather remain as she was. "The will to do and the power to think is the life of your life." *New York Times*, February 6, 1913.

10. Helen Keller, "My Future as I See it," *Ladies Home Journal*, vol. 20, November 1903; Keller, *Out of the Dark*, 114. Regarding Addams see Diliberto, *A Useful Woman*. Robyn Muncy describes college-educated women's emphasis on service in Muncy, *Creating a Female Dominion*, chapter 1.

11. Freeberg, *The Education of Laura Bridgman*, 133.

12. Keller, *My Religion*, 122.

13. Ibid., 46, 47, 122.

14. Keller, *Light in My Darkness*, 106, 107, 168.

15. Helen Keller, "What I am Doing," *Ladies Home Journal*, vol. 22, September 1905, 4.

16. Helen Keller, "My Future as I See it."

17. Gitter, *The Imprisoned Guest*; Freeberg, *The Education of Laura Bridgman*.

18. *New York Times*, May 12, 1903; January 16, 1907.

19. *New York Times*, January 16, 1907; *Outlook*, January 26, 1907; *New York Times*, February 23, 1913.

20. Helen Keller, "'I Must Speak': A Plea to the American Woman," *Ladies Home Journal*, vol. 26, January 1909.

21. Ibid.

22. Ibid. See also: Lash, *Helen and Teacher*, 365–366; *New York Times Magazine*, February 27, 1938, 13. She also wrote about the incident in *Midstream*, 79–81.

23. Keller, *Midstream*, 157; Einhorn, *Helen Keller*, 91.

24. Lash, *Helen and Teacher*, 366; Keller, *Out of the Dark*, 21; Wells, *New Worlds for Old*, 3; Arturo Giovannitti to John Macy, October 2, 1913, Arturo Giovannitti folder, Helen Keller Archives, American Foundation for the Blind (hereafter referred to as AFB).

25. Keller, *Midstream*, 34, 27–46, 83–86; Keller, *Teacher*, 105.

26. Keller, *Midstream*, 34.

27. Foner, *Helen Keller*, 27–28, 120; Lash, *Helen and Teacher*, 369, 373.

28. Foner, *Helen Keller*, 46–47, 86; Bell, *Marxian Socialism in the United States*, 68–78.

29. Foner, *Helen Keller*, 58, 89–90, 98–99; Keller, *Midstream*, 275–276; Helen Keller to John Macy, April 4, 1914, John Macy folder, AFB.

30. Keller, "The Hand of the World," *American Magazine*, vol. 75, December 1912, 44; Keller, "Blind Leaders," *Outlook*, vol. 105, September 27, 1913, 235.

31. Foner, *Helen Keller*, 37. Her support of the 1916 Wrentham, Massachusetts strike is evidenced in *New York Times*, July 8, 1916.

32. Foner, *Helen Keller*, 83–84; Snyder, "Women, Wobblies, and Workers' Rights." See also: Foner, *Helen Keller*, 57, 91–93, 94–97.

33. Einhorn, *Helen Keller*, 98. Marx said: "The Proletarians have nothing to lose but their chains. They have a world to win."

34. "Plea from Helen Keller," *New York Times*, March 2, 1906; Helen Keller, "How to be Blind," *Outlook*, vol. 82, April 28, 1906, 983; Helen Keller, "What Might be Done for the Blind," *The World's Work*, vol. 14, April 1907, 9260.

35. Helen Keller, letter to the editor, *New York Times*, October 29, 1929; Helen Keller quoted in *New York Times*, May 11, 1924, II, 2:1; Einhorn, *Helen Keller*, 82–87.

36. Einhorn, *Helen Keller*, 82–87; Keller, "What Might be Done for the Blind."

37. Klages, *Woeful Afflictions*, 43; Buchanan, *Illusions of Equality*; Longmore and Goldberger, "The League of the Physically Handicapped and the Great Depression."

38. "How the Blind May Be Helped," *Putnam's Monthly*, April 1907.

39. Thomson, *Extraordinary Bodies*, 50.

40. Baynton, "The Inspection Line."

41. Einhorn, *Helen Keller*, 82–87; Lash, *Helen and Teacher*, 363. Laura Bridgman, once she became an adult, also liked to think and claim herself economically independent. Freeberg, *The Education of Laura Bridgman*, 206.

42. For more on gender, work, and citizenship, see Kerber, *No Constitutional Right to be Ladies*, chapter 2.

43. Helen Keller to Andrew Carnegie, December 14, 1910, Andrew Carnegie file, AFB. See also Keller, *Midstream*, 140–147.

44. Keller, *Teacher*, 122; Ibid., 15.

45. Keller, *Midstream*, 146–148; Helen Keller to Mr. and Mrs. Carnegie, April 21, 1913, Andrew Carnegie file, AFB. In 1922, she wrote to Henry Ford outlining the financial difficulties she and Sullivan faced and requested money from him as well. Helen Keller to Henry Ford, September 9, 1922, Henry Ford file, AFB.

46. Joseph Barry, "At 70, New Spirit, New Freedom," *New York Times Magazine*, June 25, 1950; Keller, *Midstream*, 141.

47. Keller, *Teacher*, 126.

48. For example, see Helen Keller to John Macy, January 5, 1914, John Macy file, AFB.

49. Keller, *Midstream*, 149, 164–166, chapter 10.

50. Foner, *Helen Keller*, 33; *New York Times*, May 6, 1913. Keller's endorsement and participation in suffrage parades and rallies led by the National Woman's Party, the radical suffrage organization led by Alice Paul that picketed the White House almost daily for several years, allied her with the radical elements of the suffrage movement.

51. Foner, *Helen Keller*, 70–71. See also Keller, *Midstream*, 331–332. Keller met Sanger in 1944 and praised her highly in a private letter to Nella Braddy Henney: "I had wanted to know her for many years, and when the 'crisis' of contact came, her warm, rich personality justified my enthusiasm. She is indeed a truly great soul. Her instructive talk confirms my ideal as I picture her, despite imprisonment and calumny, choosing her own destiny and enabling unnumbered women to take independent charge of their lives and ensure the improved health and joy of their children." HK to NBH, September 18, 1944, Henney Collection, Perkins School for the Blind (hereafter referred to as HC, PSB).

52. Helen Keller, "The Modern Woman," *Metropolitan Magazine*, December, 1912. Reprinted in the *Congressional Record*, September 17, 1913. Keller's words are similar to Jane Addams. For example, Jane Addams, "Why Women Should Vote," 1910, cited in Lasch, *The Social Thought of Jane Addams*, 143–151.

53. *New York Times*, November 25, 1915; Pernick, *The Black Stork*, 55. For more on this case see Pernick, *The Black Stork*. For more on eugenics see Ladd-Taylor, "Eugenics, Sterilization and Modern Marriage in the USA"; Snyder and Mitchell, "Out of the Ashes of Eugenics"; Selden, "Eugenics and the Social Construction of Merit, Race, and Disability"; Klein, *Building a Better Race*; Pernick, *Black Stork*.

54. Pernick, *The Black Stork*, 33.

55. Ibid., 76. One wonders why Jane Addams criticized Haiselden while so many other progressive women in her circles did not: Lillian Wald (supported him), Margaret Sanger (kept quiet), Emma Goldman (kept quiet). This was one of the most widely discussed cases in radical and progressive circles. Addams, more than many of these women, wrestled as a young woman with her own usefulness. She had felt herself to be of little use anywhere and battled the internalized cultural hegemony of the uselessness of an upper-class, college-educated woman.

56. "Physicians Juries for Defective Babies," *New Republic*, December 18, 1915, 173–174; Pernick, *The Black Stork*, 32–55.

57. *New York Times*, November 25, 1915; Henry Ford to Helen Keller, November 27, 1915, Henry Ford Folder, AFB; Henry Ford to Helen Keller, November 24, 1915 telegram, Henry Ford Folder, AFB. For further information see Kraft, *The Peace Ship*.

58. Helen Keller to Henry Ford, November 30, 1915, Henry Ford Folder, AFB. Earlier that year Keller had criticized Ford's omission of women from his $5 a day salary and profit-sharing plan. *New York Times*, January 13, 1914.

59. Helen Keller to Henry Ford, undated, Henry Ford Folder, AFB. In this Keller wrote, "my heart is too full of the longing for peace to throw any word of obstruction in the way of its consummation. It is not for me to say that Mr. Ford's plan cannot succeed." Apparently, she later changed her mind, for in December she published a short piece in the New York *Call* about why the plan was "doomed to failure." Foner, *Helen Keller*, 27. Keller wrote more generally about Ford in *Midstream*, 291–294.

60. *New York Times*, October 6, 1918; *New York Times*, October 14, 1918; Foner, *Helen Keller*, 75–81; Keller, *Midstream*, 172. See also: *New York Times*, December 20, 1915.

61. Foner, *Helen Keller*, 73; *New York Times*, December 20, 1915.

62. Helen Keller to Henry Ford, undated, Henry Ford Folder, AFB.

63. *The Crisis*, April 1916, 305–306. See also Lash, *Helen and Teacher*, 454–456; Herrmann, *Helen Keller*, 204.

64. *The Crisis*, April 1916, 305–306; Lash, *Helen and Teacher*, 454; Herrmann, *Helen Keller*, 204.

65. Keller, *Midstream*, 220; Herrmann, *Helen Keller*, 205; Lash, *Helen and Teacher*, 454–455. Keller encountered Selma and its racial politics again at an undated point later in life. According to her biographer Van Wyck Brooks, "Du Bois had followed her career, and he had not been surprised when she spoke out frankly in Alabama against what she had called the iniquity of the colour line. It was at a public meeting in Selma, and a Negro-baiter asked Helen if she had given money for the defense of Negroes. When she answered 'Yes,' he asked her further, 'Do you believe in marriage between whites and Negroes?' To this she replied. 'No more than they do.' Then she refused to shake hands with the man, for 'I saw at once what he was,' she said to me this afternoon. She shocked her own family, along with the other Alabamians, but 'They have forgotten it,' she added." Brooks, *Helen Keller*, 138.

66. *Chicago Tribune*, June 9, 1916.

67. Keller, *Midstream*, 177–182; Herrmann, *Helen Keller*, 198. Keller's mother Kate Keller was particularly opposed to a possible marriage, and any form of a sexual life, for Helen. For fictional reflection on the Fagan incident, see Georgina Kleege, "Helen Keller's Love Life."

68. Lash, *Helen and Teacher*, 452.

59. Helen Keller, "If You Have Friends You Can Endure Anything," *American Magazine*, September 1929, 171; Keller, *Midstream*, 132–134. In 1938, Keller referred to herself as one "whom fate has denied a husband and the joy of motherhood," but it's never clear whether fate is determined by chance or her disability. Helen Keller, "She is Not Dead," *Good Housekeeping*, February 1938, 35.

70. *New York Times*, August 17, 1919; *New York Times*, August 18, 1919; *New York Times*, August 19, 1919. Keller describes *Deliverance* in *Midstream*, 186–208. For further analysis of *Deliverance*, see Cohen, "Helen Keller and the American Myth"; Crutchfield, "The Most Wonderful Woman in the World."

71. Keller describes vaudeville in *Midstream*, 209–215.

72. The most recent biography of Helen Keller equally devalues Keller's political interests by explaining them, not as ideology or genuine interest, but as "an acceptable outlet for the rage and anger that she seldom permitted herself to express about the fate that had left her disabled and helpless." Herrmann, *Helen Keller*, 175, 204. For more on civic fitness, see Nielsen, "Helen Keller and the Politics of Civic Fitness."

73. Keller, *Out of the Dark*, 20. Sullivan disagreed with Keller's politics. She was never a suffragist, or a socialist. In the above 1913 essay Keller wrote, "Perhaps she will be one before Mr. Macy and I have done arguing with her." A 1913 *New York Times* interview asked Keller the question explicitly of whether her political views were gained from Anne Sullivan. *New York Times*, February 6, 1913.

74. Keller, *Out of the Dark*, 20; Keller, *Teacher*, 15.

75. This is, as far as I can determine, the only time Keller used the word "right" in reference to herself.

76. Keller, "Blind Leaders," *Outlook*, vol. 105, September 27, 1913, 231; Foner, *Helen Keller*, 52–54, 75–81.

77. Keller, "Blind Leaders," 231–232.

78. Keller, *Out of the Dark*, 30.

79. Ibid., 178.

80. Ibid., 67.

81. Ibid., 76.

82. Goldman, *Living My Life*, 648–649.

NOTES TO CHAPTER 2

1. Lash, *Helen and Teacher*, 517, chapter 29. What interested Migel in blindness is not clear. Having made a fortune by his forties, he was already involved in education for blind people and easily moved to leadership in the AFB.

2. Lash, *Helen and Teacher*, 524–529.

3. Ibid., 530–531; Keller, *Midstream*, 232.

4. Koestler, *The Unseen Minority*, see chapter 2. For examples of antiradicalism see Nielsen, *Un-American Womanhood*. Though Anne and John Macy initially were blamed for Keller's activism, Anne never approved of Keller's socialism, suffrage advocacy, or other political interests. Her disapproval may have been compounded by the fact that Keller was first introduced to radicalism by Macy, her estranged husband. Herrmann, *Helen Keller*, 178, 204–205; Lash, *Helen and Teacher*, 454–455.

5. Foner, *Helen Keller*, 113. See also *New York Times*, August 6, 1924; *New York Times*, October 1, 1924; Helen Keller to "Dear Mrs. La Follette," September 1, 1924, La Follette Family Papers, Library of Congress, Belle Case La Follette—special correspondence, Helen Keller (box D16). For further information on La Follette, see Unger, *Fighting Bob La Follette*. Keller used the same words in *Midstream*, 172–173 and described her admiration for La Follette, 276–277.

6. For a discussion of the medicalization of disability, see Bogdan, *Freak Show*, 278. For more on immigration see Baynton, "The Inspection Line"; Baynton, "Disability and the Justification of Inequality in American History."

7. Einhorn, *Helen Keller*, 23. M. C. Migel, president of the American Foundation for the Blind, tried in 1949 to convince Eleanor Roosevelt to use her influence to allow Keller to address the United Nations Assembly on "labors to be undertaken on behalf of the sightless of the world." M. C. Migel to Eleanor Roosevelt, January

19, 1949, Roosevelt folder, AFB. In 1960, former labor leader Mary Elisabeth Dreier wrote to Keller: "When you went abroad, and to the east, I had thought what a wonderful thing it would be if they made you an Ambassador of the United States. The government has been insensitive, and normally would be, I presume to such an idea." Mary E. Dreier to Helen Keller, July 13, 1960, Mary Elisabeth Dreier Papers, box 10, folder 166, Schlesinger Library.

8. For example, see Koestler, *Unseen Minority*, chapter 6.

9. Keller, *Midstream*, 248.

10. *New York Times*, January 7, 1928; January 12, 1928. Men such as John D. Rockefeller, Felix Warburg, and M. C. Migel's donations of $50,000 apiece were noted by the *New York Times*. The Endowment had been planned since Macy and Keller agreed to join AFB in 1924.

11. *New York Times*, October 29, 1929. Keller adopted a similar strategy in a 1957 appeal for the American Overseas Blind. *New York Times*, December 7, 1957.

12. Joseph Lash's interview with Robert Barnett, Joseph Lash Papers, box 53, folder 7, Franklin and Eleanor Roosevelt Library (hereafter referred to as FERL).

13. *New York Times*, November 24, 1931; April 10, 1940; April 30, 1941; May 13, 1949. The Jewish women's organization Hadassah reciprocated by honoring Keller. They did so in 1947 by giving her an "honorary" membership. *New York Times*, October 14, 1947.

14. *New York Times*, June 18, 1942; October 19, 1927; June 27, 1947. See also: June 27, 1947 speech by Helen Keller, Speeches Given by Helen Keller, AFB; April 8, 1961 speech by Helen Keller, Speeches Given by Helen Keller, AFB.

15. Address by M. C. Migel, November 14, 1932, M. C. Migel folder, AFB.

16. These include Arkansas (1945), Colorado (1925), Delaware (1931 or 1932), Florida (1929, 1941), Hawaii (1937), Illinois (1931), Iowa (1924), Maine (1939), Mississippi (1929, 1941, 1942), Nebraska (1947), New Jersey (1934), New Mexico (1925, 1941), North Carolina (1935), North Dakota (1933), Texas (1941), Utah (1941), Vermont (1929), Virginia (1924). I suspect this list is fairly incomplete.

17. For example, see: Virginia Association of Workers for the Blind, Inc. to Helen Keller, 1924, Legislation: state, General, AFB; Ruth Pratt to Helen Keller, March 3, 1931, Legislation: Federal, Library Services for the Blind, AFB; Russell Tyson to Helen Keller, May 1, 1931, Legislation: state, General, AFB; B.P. Chapple to Helen Keller, March 20, 1933, Legislation: state, General, AFB.

18. Helen Keller to Franklin Delano Roosevelt, May 19, 1933, Legislation: Federal-General, AFB; M.C. Migel to Helen Keller, February 15, 1932, Legislation: state, General, AFB; Bob Irwin to Helen Keller, February 27, 1937, Legislation: Federal, Library Services for the Blind, AFB.

19. Helen Keller to Thomas Cullen, June 21, 1935, Legislation-Federal, Social Security Act-Title X, AFB; Helen Keller to Robert Doughton, June 21, 1935, Legislation-Federal, Social Security Act-Title X, AFB; *New York Times*, June 16, 1935. For the Deaf community's response to the Social Security Act of 1935, see Buchanan, *Illusions of Equality*, 96.

20. Helen Keller's speech before the House Labor Committee Investigating Aid to the Handicapped, October 3, 1944, Legislation-Federal, Social Security Act-Title X, AFB. See also *New York Times*, October 4, 1944.

21. Bob Barnett to Helen Keller, December 8, 1943, Legislation: Federal, General, AFB; Helen Keller to Robert Barnett, December 9, 1943, Legislation: Federal, General, AFB; Robert Barnett to Helen Keller, December 13, 1943, Legislation: Federal, Insurance Against Blindness, AFB.

22. Helen Keller to Nella Braddy Henney, undated letter from "late 1920s," Henney folder, AFB. Later Nella wrote on this letter that Keller was probably referring to *My Religion*.

23. Herrmann, *Helen Keller*, 269.

24. Lash, *Helen and Teacher*, 553; Keller, *My Religion*, 157.

25. Lash, *Helen and Teacher*, 560–561.

26. Keller, *Midstream*, 6; Lash, *Helen and Teacher*, 566.

27. Lash, *Helen and Teacher*, 587; Keller, *Teacher*, 180–181.

28. Keller, *Teacher*, 79, 198–199.

29. Ibid., 159.

30. Helen Keller to Nella Braddy Henney, May 5, 1932, Henney folder, AFB; *New York Times*, October 19, 1932.

31. Helen Keller, "The Great Choice," *Home Magazine*, January 1932, Writings by Helen Keller, AFB; *New York Times*, February 1, 1932. See also "Women and Peace," *Home Magazine*, May 1930, Writings by Helen Keller, AFB.

32. *New York Times*, May 10, 1933; May 11, 1933. The reportedly burned book was *Out of the Dark*. She had learned of the burning from Cornelius Vanderbilt, Jr. The inclusion of her books was disputed in 1934. *New York Times*, April 10, 1934.

33. *New York Times*, September 20, 1934; September 29, 1934. See also: *The American*, September 20, 1934.

34. She went on to quote the Bible, "Better were it for you to have a millstone hung around your neck and sink into the sea than to be hated and despised of all men." *New York Times*, May 10, 1933.

35. Letters between Polly Thomson and Amelia Bond, May 22, 1930, July 3, 1930, July 9, 1930, July 31, 1930, Amelia Bond folder, AFB; *New York Times Review*, June 1, 1930, 19.

36. Macy, *About Women*, 18, 85; Herrmann, *Helen Keller*, 253.

37. Lash, *Helen and Teacher*, 607–609. The initial members of the Helen Keller Trust were Migel, Harvey Gibson, and William Ziegler. Lash, *Helen and Teacher*, 619, 648; Herrmann, *Helen Keller*, 231.

38. Keller, *Helen Keller's Journal*, 9, 35; Keller, *My Religion*, 102; Keller, *Teacher*, 139.

39. Keller, *Helen Keller's Journal*, 80, 83.

40. Keller, *Teacher*, 222. Nella Braddy Henney told the same story: Henney, *With Helen Keller*, 7. Lash, *Helen and Teacher*, 636.

41. Keller, *Helen Keller's Journal*, 54, 88.

42. Ibid., 155, 189.

44. Ibid., 203, 217–223.

44. Keller wrote in 1956 that "not until after Polly and I had made our voyage to Japan on the *Asama-Maru* did a spark of self-activity begin to illuminate the void for me." Keller, *Teacher*, 228; Lash, *Helen and Teacher*, 637.

45. Keller, *Helen Keller's Journal*, 255, 262; *New York Times*, March 21, 1937; March 26, 1937.

46. Keller, *Helen Keller's Journal*, 283, see April 1937 entries.

47. Ibid., 293, 295–296.

NOTES TO CHAPTER 3

1. Lash, *Helen and Teacher*, 643–645. Thomson had a different impression of the Buddha. She wrote that "Nara goes back 1200 years. Helen and I touched the famous bronze Buddha seated on lotus leaves, the only two women ever to touch and get near that sacred figure. It was a dusty, tiresome business. Oh, oh, the things a celebrity has to do. Poor Helen! But she is always so sweet and marvelous about it." Excerpts from letters from HK and PT from Japan [retyped in files], Foreign Travels 1937, Japan, AFB.

2. HK to "Dear Elsie," April 10, 1937 (daughter of Alexander Graham Bell, who was married to Gilbert H. Grosvenor), Grosvenor Family Papers, Library of Congress; Clipping from *The Japan Advertiser*, April 23, 1937, HK, President's Personal File #2169, FERL; Taiichi Hara, Exec secretary of the [Japanese] National Association for the Blind to Migel, May 30, 1937, Foreign travels 1937, Japan, AFB.

3. HK to John Finley, July 14, 1937, John H. and Martha Finley folder, AFB.

4. Clipping from *The Japan Advertiser*, July 6, 1937, HK, President's Personal File #2169, FERL; May 1, 1937 Report No. 2393, "Visit to Japan of Miss Helen Keller," to the Secretary of State from Joseph C. Grew, HK, President's Personal File 2169,

FERL. Grew went on to say, "There could be no better illustration of the latent sentiment in the character of the Japanese people than the spontaneous welcome accorded by the Japanese, high and low, to Miss Helen Keller, famous educator of the deaf, dumb, and blind. The sentimentalism and superficial politeness of the Japanese are well-known, but on this occasion their real sentiment was strikingly displayed."

5. Lash, *Helen and Teacher*, 645; HK to Migel, September 14, 1937, Migel folder, AFB; HK to John Finley, July 14, 1937, John H. and Martha Finley folder, AFB; *New York Times*, August 10, 1937.

In April 1937, she wrote to Elsie Grosvenor that "how tragically far off permanent PEACE seems at present with China and Japan at each other's throats! All my democratic sympathies are with China, but I am afraid that disorganized nation, with many voices of counsel and few voices of vision, doing many things but nothing well, must go through cruel defeats and long discipline before it emerges triumphant among the commonwealths of the world." HK to "Dear Elsie," April 10, 1937, Grosvenor Family Personal Files, Library of Congress. Literary rights given to the public.

6. HK to Migel, September 14, 1937, Migel folder, AFB.

7. HK, "She is Not Dead," *Good Housekeeping*, February 2, 1938, 144.

8. "Helen Keller Makes Dramatic Plea for Baby," *New York Daily Mirror*, May 9, 1938; "Save Doomed Baby, Helen Keller Pleads," *New York Journal American*, May 8, 1938; "Conscientious Doctors Possess High Courage," *New York World-Telegram*, May 10, 1938; all clippings in the Nella Braddy Henney Journal, Henney Collection, Perkins School for the Blind (hereafter referred to as HJ), HC, PSB.

9. "Save Doomed Baby, Helen Keller Pleads."

10. "Helen Keller Makes Dramatic Plea for Baby."

11. *New York Times*, July 19, 1938. Keller knew the Roosevelts well enough to know that for a message to reach FDR quickly or to be considered seriously it was best to go through Missy LeHand, FDR's private secretary. When Anne Sullivan died, Keller telegrammed LeHand with the funeral information. Telegram from HK to Missy LeHand, October 20, 1936, President's Personal File #2169, HK, FERL.

12. Report of Purchases Made Under the Schedule of Blind-Made Products, May 27, 1940, FDR Papers as President, Official File, #3303, Committee on Purchase of Products Made by the Blind, FERL; Koestler, *Unseen Minority*, 219.

13. HK to Franklin Roosevelt, July 15, 1938, FDR Papers as President, Official File, #3303, Committee on Purchase of Products Made by the Blind, FERL.

14. Keller, *Midstream*, 87–88; HK to Migel, July 1938, Migel folder, AFB.

15. HK to Walter Holmes, November 19, 1938, Walter Holmes file, AFB.

16. HK to John Finley, December 2, 1938, Finley folder, AFB. After seeing *The Diary of Anne Frank* in 1955 with Keller, NBJ reported that HK was strongly affected: "It was very moving and we all felt drained and weak as we made our way to the Harvard Club for dinner. Helen said, 'I felt my deaf-blind friend very close to me throughout the play.' She referred to a deaf-blind woman who was destroyed in one of the concentration camps. I sat next to Helen and could feel the intensity of her emotion in the tenseness of the muscles in her hands and arms, but she began to relax when we ordered drinks." HJ, December 28, 1955, HC, PSB. Keller may have been referring to the poetess. As far as I've been able to discover, Finley and the *New York Times* did not do the editorial Keller requested.

17. HK to Walter Holmes, May 17, 1939, Walter Holmes folder, AFB; *New York Times*, August 15, 1939; HK to Walter Holmes, May 9, 1941, Walter Holmes file, AFB.

18. *New York Times*, November 16, 1940; December 5, 1940; January 7, 1941; January 8, 1941; January 9, 1941. For examples of Keller's appeals, see: HK to Frieda Miller, December 16, 1940, Frieda Segelke Miller Collection, Schlesinger Library; HK to Eleanor Roosevelt, November 12, 1940, Eleanor Roosevelt Papers, White House Correspondence, series 20.9, FERL; HK to Eleanor Roosevelt, December 1, 1940, Eleanor Roosevelt Papers, series 95, FERL.

19. *New York Times*, February 8, 1941. See also *New York Times*, February 9, 1941. Military Intelligence Division of the War Department, National Archives. Keller does not have an official FBI file but is cross-referenced extensively in the files of other individuals and organizations. My 1997 appeal for information on Keller, under the Freedom of Information Act, netted a review of 118 pages and the release of 44 pages. See also Pelka, "Helen Keller and the FBI."

20. HK to Walter Holmes, December 19, 1941, Walter Holmes file, AFB.

21. Migel to Mr. Charles A. Thomson, November 19, 1941, HK Foreign Travels, 1942 South America, Planning: State Department, AFB; Harry Pierson, State Department, to Migel, November 21, 1941, Foreign Travels, 1942 South America, Planning-State Department, AFB; November 25, 1941 letter from Migel to Pierson, November 25, 1941, Foreign Travels, 1942 South America, Planning-State Department, AFB.

The records of the State Department provide incredible information about Keller's international activities after World War II. I had the thrill of blowing nearly sixty years of dust off, slowly opening creaking files that no one had looked at since they were first submitted to the State Department.

22. Harry Pierson, State Department, to Migel, December 10, 1941, Foreign Travels, 1942 South America, Planning-State Department, AFB; Harry Pierson,

State Department, to Migel, January 2, 1941, Foreign Travels, 1942 South America, Planning-State Department, AFB; Migel to HK, February 16, 1942, Foreign Travels, 1942 South America, Planning-State Department, AFB.

23. Keller, *The Story of My Life*, 20.

24. HK to NBH, June 23, 1950, Henney folder, AFB; Davidson, *Between Sittings*, 333; Jo Davidson to HK, March 6, 1948, Papers of Jo Davidson, Jo Davidson Collection, Library of Congress. See also Brooks, *Helen Keller*, chapter 9.

25. HK to Clare Heineman, April 28, 1943, Claire and Oscar Heineman file, AFB; HK to Guthrie McClintic, May 1, 1943, Katharine Cornell file, AFB.

Jo and Florence Davidson frequently provided such events. In 1944, she described an evening with them as such: "Not long afterwards we had one of our magical evenings dining with Jo and Florence at the studio. Among their guests were Lin Yutang and his wife Madame Hong, a dear, warm-hearted woman whom he calls 'the real spirit of China.'—How I wish the Fates had appointed her instead of Madame Chiang to represent the suffering heroic nation! Mr. VanWyck Brooks too was there. He is at present engaged in the supreme effort of his life—writing a history of American literature. And we also met Bob Flaherty, the producer of the marvelous films 'Sabu the Elephant-boy,' and pictures of South Sea Islanders and Eskimos. It was an event for me to be at that gathering of brilliant minds and listen to talk from which sparks fell on every subject—China, books, Roosevelt and Dewey, philosophy, Russia and postwar Reconstruction. The only element lacking to make my satisfaction complete was Teacher's presence, she delighted in inspiring discussions, sallies of wit and large views of world affairs." HK to Clare Heineman, June 6, 1944, Oscar and Clare Heineman file, AFB.

26. HK to NBH, January 4, 1943, Henney folder, AFB.

27. Ibid.

28. *New York Times*, August 24, 1944; HK to NBH, September 18, 1944, HC, PSB. See also November 18, 1930, FDR folder, AFB; November 30, 1932, FDR folder, AFB; November 2, 1935, FDR folder, AFB; *New York Times*, September 20, 1934; January 27, 1942; August 24, 1944; September 22, 19—. In 1933, Keller privately expressed some reticence about FDR, fearing that elements of the New Deal were "autocratic." HK to Migel, August 21, 1933, Migel file, AFB.

29. HK to Walter Holmes, February 13, 1945, Walter Holmes file, AFB. She used almost the same words in a letter to Clare and Oscar Heineman, February 8, 1945, Clare and Oscar Heineman file, AFB.

30. *New York Times*, December 11, 1942; December 12, 1942; December 27, 1942; NBH to PT, April 24, 1943, April 28, 1943, HC, PSB. Keller toured limited veteran hospitals in World War I. See *New York Times*, June 22, 1916; June 23, 1916.

31. Helen Keller, "Deaf but Not Down!" *Rotarian*, November 1944, 15; *New York Times*, November 11, 1944. See also *New York Times*, February 8, 1945; *New York Times*, April 24, 1945.

Personally, Keller was astounded by the changes in the medical practices of rehabilitation. To Walter Holmes she wrote, "As I look back upon the recent tour, it startles me as an experience too poignant and tremendous to compass within the limited medium of prose. It is an epic beside which all Iliads and Aeneids seem pale and insular. As Polly and I traveled through Arkansas, Oklahoma, Texas, New Mexico, Colorado, Utah, California, Oregon and Washington State, we were kept highstrung by the miracles we witnessed in healing the wounded and reclaiming the disabled. Hospitals which would once have been places of heartbreak are now bright with a dynamic faith and the purpose it inspires. Surgeons, physicians, scientists and rehabilitation workers are striving towards an unprecedented goal—restoring multitudes of injured servicemen to normal society and usefulness to an extent that has never been possible before in the history of the world." HK to Walter Holmes, February 13, 1945, Walter Holmes file, AFB.

32. HK to Jo Davidson, November 11, 1945, Jo Davidson Collection, Library of Congress.

33. HK to Walter Holmes, November 19, 1938, Walter Holmes file, AFB; HK to Walter Holmes, June 11, 1941, Walter Holmes file, AFB; HK to Walter Holmes, May 9, 1941, Walter Holmes file, AFB; HK to Walter Holmes, June 11, 1941, Walter Holmes file, AFB.

34. HK to Walter Holmes, June 11, 1941, Walter Holmes file, AFB; HK's speech before the House Labor Committee Investigating Aid to the Handicapped, October 3, 1944, Legislation-Federal, Social Security Act-Title X, AFB. See also *New York Times*, October 4, 1944; *New York Times*, June 28, 1945; June 29, 1945.

35. HK to NBH, September 18, 1944, HC, PSB.

36. Ibid.

37. HK to Jo Davidson, April 22, 1945, Jo Davidson Collection, Library of Congress. To Clare and Oscar Heineman she wrote, "the catastrophe seemed to me like a fruitful continent vanishing under the ocean, bearing down with it newly garnered stores of bread and healing for the nation. Personally I shall miss Roosevelt's unfailing sympathy which was a pilgrim staff in my hand as I sought wider opportunities for the handicapped." HK to Clare and Oscar Heineman, July 11, 1945, Clare and Oscar Heineman file, AFB.

38. HK to Takeo Iwahashi, March 11, 1946, Iwahashi file, AFB.

39. HK to NBH, September 22, 1946, Henney Correspondence file, HC, PSB;

New York Times, December 22, 1946; January 17, 1947; April 18, 1947; May 6, 1947; June 28, 1947; January 23, 1948.

40. HK to NBH, September 22, 1946, Henney Correspondence file, HC, PSB; HJ, November/December 1946, HC, PSB.

41. Lash, *Helen and Teacher*, 696–699.

42. HJ, February 17, 1947, HC, PSB.

43. HK to Eric Boulter, February 10, 1947, Eric Boulter file, AFB; HK to NBH, September 22, 1946, HC, PSB; Lash, *Helen and Teacher*, 683, 690–707; Herrmann, *Helen Keller*, 282.

44. A lengthy description of the evening is found in HJ, March 31, 1947, HC, PSB.

45. HJ, February 25, 1947, HC, PSB; Henney's thoughts on the Westbrook Pegler column are in her journal, HJ, December 17, 1947, HC, PSB.

46. Lash, *Helen and Teacher*, 702–704; HJ, February 26, 1948, HC, PSB.

47. HK to Migel, January 12, 1947, Migel file, AFB.

48. HK to Migel, November 3, 1947, Migel file, AFB; Lash, *Helen and Teacher*, 708.

49. HK to Jo Davidson, March 6, 1948, Papers of Jo Davidson, Library of Congress.

50. HJ, November/December 1948, HC, PSB.

51. Ibid.; Nelson Neff, "Travels with Helen and Polly"; Lash, *Helen and Teacher*, 709–710.

52. HJ, November/December 1948, HC, PSB.

53. Dower, *Embracing Defeat*, 23.

54. Yukisaburo Takeda to HK, February 16, 1948, Foreign Travel, 1948 Japan, AFB.

55. Lash, *Helen and Teacher*, 710–711; *New York Times*, September 5, 1948; Takeo Iwahashi to Col. Sams, October 28, 1948, Iwahashi file, AFB; 1948 Farewell speech, October 23, 1948, Japan, AFB.

56. Osaka speech to social workers, 1948, Iwahashi file, AFB; Address to women, Foreign Travel, 1948 Japan, AFB; October 23, 1948 press conference speech, Foreign Travel, 1948 Japan, AFB.

57. Hiroshima speech 1948, Iwahashi file, AFB.

58. Henney and Davidson considered pursuing U.S. publication of the letter. Jo Davidson to NBH, December 20, 1948, Papers of Jo Davidson, Library of Congress. In 1975 the AFB sought publication of the letter in the *Saturday Review* or *Atlantic Monthly* but was rejected. Japan file, AFB.

59. Copy of HK to NBH, October 14, 1948, Papers of Jo Davidson, Library of Congress.

60. Ibid.

61. Ibid.; Nagai, *The Bells of Nagasaki*; Dower, *Embracing Defeat*, 198.

62. 1948 Farewell speech, October 23, 1948, Japan, AFB; Copy of HK to NBH, October 14, 1948, Papers of Jo Davidson, Library of Congress.

63. Copy of HK to NBH, October 14, 1948, Papers of Jo Davidson, Library of Congress.

64. HJ, December 29, 1949, HC, PSB. In 1950, Keller and Thomson made preliminary attempts to adopt Hiroshima orphans: "H and P, acting under Norman Cousins' impulse are trying to adopt Hiroshima orphans, one each." HJ, January 5, 1950, HC, PSB.

65. Klages, *Woeful Afflictions*, 193. For more on authorial selfhood, see 190–194.

66. Copy of HK to NBH, October 14, 1948, Papers of Jo Davidson, Library of Congress.

67. HK to Clare Heineman, July 5, 1946, Oscar and Clare Heineman file, AFB. In 1954, Takeo Iwahashi wrote her about the continued U.S. hydrogen bomb experiments at Bikini Island. No record remains of Keller's response. "You remember, Helen's most sincere looking when you both listened to the Mayor of Hiroshima's explanation upon the awful damage of the city by the first atomic bombing. Japan again is terribly shocked by the hydrogen bombing, which was experimented recently at the Bikini Island. It is more than you imagine how we hate such a cruel weapon, that was invented by your Army specialists. Alas! 'No more Hiroshima' is going to be an empty echo of the last war. We pacifists now must stand such a demonical instrument beyond classes and barriers of the nation. As I know how you were strong enough to fight against the militarism during the first war, it is a time for you to cry again for peace and reasoning in the sacred name of humanity in order to save the world from total destruction. Mrs. Roosevelt who came to Japan last year gave us a very good impression as a real humanist representing the most intelligent cosmopolitan women of America. It is my sincere desire particularly at this critical period to get Helen's heavenly voice as messenger of real peace and love in a written form to the coming Japanese blind Assembly at Hiroshima." Takeo Iwahashi to HK, April 14, 1954, Iwahashi file, AFB.

68. Chikao Honda and Yoshitaro Kusuyama, managing editor and editor-in-chief of *The Mainichi*, to HK and PT, October 23, 1948, Foreign Travel, 1948 Japan, AFB; Osaka Municipal Assembly, September 30, 1948, Foreign Travel, 1948 Japan, AFB; Hajime Sato to HK, December 23, 1948, Foreign Travel, 1948 Japan, AFB;

Juzo Tsukamoto, Chairman of Welfare Committee, Japanese House of Councillors, to HK, November 21, 1959, Foreign Travel, 1948 Japan, AFB.

69. October 13, 1948 welcome address of Mayor of Hiroshima, Shinzo Hamai, to HK, Foreign Travel, 1948 Japan, AFB; Laurence Critchell, "The Day Helen Keller Came to Tokyo," *Saturday Evening Post*, February 25, 1956, 31–35. Nella Braddy Henney loved this article. "We all had been enchanted," HJ, February 23, 1956, HC, PSB.

70. HK to Col. Sams, November 3, 1948, Japan, AFB.

71. George C. Marshall to the Embassy in Manila, June 11, 1948, General Records of the Department of State, 1948–1949. Central Decimal File, 032. Keller, Helen, 1945–1949; Emmet O'Neal, US Ambassador to the Philippines, to HK, September 30, 1948, Foreign Travel, 1948 Japan, AFB.

NOTES TO CHAPTER 4

1. March 8, 1948, April 8, 1948, May 20, 1948. No. 40. General Records of the State Department, 1945–1949 Central Decimal File. 032 HK.

2. Keller, *My Religion*, 137.

3. Lash, *Helen and Teacher*, 720–721; HK to "Dear Jo and Florence," July 24, 1950, Papers of Jo Davidson, Library of Congress.

4. Undated letter from HK to Jo Davidson (the first written since Herbert's death), Papers of Jo Davidson, Library of Congress; Lash, *Helen and Teacher*, 714–718, 722.

5. Robert Barnett to Mr. Harry Simmons, Executive Director, Florida Council for the Blind, November 30, 1950, Helen Keller Archives-Awards, AFB.

6. Lash, *Helen and Teacher*, 722–725; HK to Jo Davidson, January 24, 1951, Davidson file, AFB. See also Blaxall, *Helen Keller under the Southern Cross*, 32–33.

7. HK to Jo Davidson, January 24, 1951, Jo Davidson file, AFB.

8. Lash, *Helen and Teacher*, 724; Blaxall, *Helen Keller under the Southern Cross*, 47; *New York Times*, February 8, 1951.

9. Blaxall, *Helen Keller under the Southern Cross*, 16, 25, 51; HK to Takeo Iwahashi, August 5, 1951, Iwahashi file, AFB.

10. Undated 1951 newspaper article, HJ, HC, PSB; Blaxall, *Helen Keller under the Southern Cross*, 36, 51.

11. HK to Takeo Iwahashi, August 5, 1951, Iwahashi file, AFB; HK to Jo Davidson, 1951 (no further date), Jo Davidson file, AFB; HK to Alexander Graham Bell, March 9, 1900, Alexander Graham Bell Collection, Library of Congress.

12. HJ, January 10, 1952, HC, PSB; Lash, *Helen and Teacher*, 725–728.

13. HJ, January 8, 1952, HC, PSB; Lash, *Helen and Teacher*, 728.

14. HJ, January 10, 1952, February 20, 1952, March 14, 1952, HC, PBS; NBH to Lenore Smith, April 15, 1952, Philip and Lenore Smith folder, AFB.

15. February 8, 1952 Office memorandum from NE-S. P. Dorsey to NE-Mr. S. K. C. Kopper, General Records of the Department of State, 1950–1954 Central Decimal File. 032 HK; March 13, 1952 airgram from Dept of State, Dean Acheson to American Diplomatic Officers re: HK and PT trip to Near East, General Records of the Department of State, 1950–1954 Central Decimal File. 032 HK.

16. February 8, 1952 Office memorandum from NE-S. P. Dorsey to NE-Mr. S. K. C. Kopper, General Records of the Department of State, 1950–1954 Central Decimal File. 032 HK; February 15, 1952 from J. Paul Barringer, Acting Director, Office of Transport and Communications Policy, to Mr. Donald W. Nyrop (Civil Aeronautics Board, Dept of Commerce), General Records of the Department of State, 1950–1954 Central Decimal File. 032 HK.

17. April 1, 1952 from William L. Thorp, Assistant Secretary of State to Donald Nyrop, Chair, Civil Aeronautics Board, General Records of the Department of State, 1950–1954 Central Decimal File. 032 HK. See also Eric Boulter, Field Director, AFOB to Mr. Samuel K.C. Kopper, Deputy Director, Near East Affairs, Department of State, April 16, 1952, General Records of the Department of State, 1950–1954 Central Decimal File. 032 HK; NEA-Mr. Berry to E-Mr. Thorp, March 24, 1952, General Records of the Department of State, 1950–1954 Central Decimal File. 032 HK.

18. Cairo Embassy to Dept of State, April 17, 1952, General Records of the Department of State, 1950–1954, Central Decimal File. 032 HK; HK to NBH, July 2, 1952, Henney folder, AFB. Information on this trip is necessarily guided by sources. Unfortunately, the Embassy reports are not uniform in size or detail. More is known about the time in Jordan than anywhere else.

19. American Embassy, Cairo to State Dept from C. Robert Payne, Public Affairs Officer, April 30, 1952, General Records of the Department of State, 1950–1954 Central Decimal File. 032 HK; Rubin, *Secrets of State*, 88–89.

20. HK to NBH, July 2, 1952, Henney folder, AFB; American Embassy, Damascus to State Department, June 2, 1952, General Records of the Department of State, 1950–1954, Central Decimal File. 032 HK.

21. Ibid.

22. Foreign Service Dispatch from American Embassy, Amman, Jordan to State Department, May 13, 1952, General Records of the Department of State, 1950–1954, Central Decimal File. 032 HK.

23. Report on HK's visit to Arab Jerusalem from Richard Parker, American Vice Consul to Dept of State, May 16, 1952, General Records of the Department of State, 1950–1954, Central Decimal File. 032 HK.

24. HK to NBH, July 2, 1952, Henney folder, AFB; *New York Times*, May 27, 1952.

25. HK to NBH, July 2, 1952, Henney folder, AFB.

26. Ibid.

27. Berghahn, "Philanthropy and Diplomacy in the 'American Century.'"

28. HJ, August 28, 1952, November 19, 1952, HC, PSB.

29. *New York Times*, August 28, 1952. See also HJ, August 28, 1952, HC, PSB. Biographer Dorothy Herrmann notes that Keller's disability also made her a difficult person for the FBI to watch. Her conversations were impossible to monitor and wiretapping her phone would have been virtually useless. Herrmann, *Helen Keller*, 283.

30. This film was known as both *The Unconquered* and *Helen Keller—in her Story*.

31. HJ, November 29, 1952, HC, PSB.

32. The meeting included Henney, Keller, Robert Flaherty, Polly Thomson, and AFB publicity director Mrs. Stevens and AFB staff member Dick Whittington. HJ, January 19, 1950, HC, PSB.

33. HJ, January 30–31, 1950, HC, PSB; Lash, *Helen and Teacher*, 665, 744–746. Hamilton was Cornell's manager and friend. Discussions of the film in Henney's journal begin in March 1952 and continue throughout the 1950s. HJ, HC, PSB.

34. HJ, November 29, 1952, HC, PSB.

35. Lash, *Helen and Teacher*, 732–738.

36. Airgram from Dept of State (John Foster Dulles) to American Diplomatic officers, May 4, 1953, General Records of the Department of State, 1950–1954, Central Decimal File. 032 HK. Brazil: John W. Campbell, Public Affairs Officer, to State Department, June 9, 1953, General Records of the Department of State, 1950–1954, Central Decimal File. 032 HK; Peru: Thomas T. Driver, Public Affairs Officer, to State Department, June 11, 1953, General Records of the Department of State, 1950–1954, Central Decimal File. 032 HK; Mexico: Robert G. Caldwell, Cultural Advisor to the Ambassador, U.S. Embassy, Mexico, July 1, 1953, General Records of the Department of State, 1950–1954, Central Decimal File. 032 HK.

37. HJ, August 25, 1953, HC, PSB.

38. Nelson Neff to Eric Boulter, September 11, 1953, Neff folder, AFB; Nelson Neff to PT, September 11, 1953, Neff folder, AFB; Eric Boulter to Nelson Neff, January 5, 1954, Awards-Nobel Prize, AFB. See the AFB's Nobel Prize folder for general information. Keller left no evidence of her opinion of the Nobel Prize efforts, but

certainly she knew of it. Henney wrote in her journal that "Helen showed no interest in the talk about the Nobel Prize. Honors truly mean nothing to her. She said that when she got to heaven she was going to be one of the fortunate ones whose task it will be to work for the truth." HJ, February 20, 1952, HC, PSB.

39. Letter to Members of the World Council for the Welfare of the Blind (WCWB) from the Japanese Representative members to the W.C.W.B., April 3, 1958, Awards-Nobel Prize, AFB. Dulles apparently could not because the U.S. government could not make an official nomination. Hulen C. Walker to Eric Boulter, February 1, 1954, Awards-Nobel Prize, AFB; Eric T. Boulter to the Nobel Peace Prize Committee, January 27, 1954, Awards-Nobel Prize, AFB.

40. Lash, *Helen and Teacher*, 746.

41. HJ, November 9–12, 1954, HC, PSB.

42. *New York Times*, February 2, 1955; February 1, 1955 Farewell Dinner, General, Foreign Travel, AFB. To Eleanor Roosevelt, she wrote that night: "The beautiful words you addressed to me last night went straight to my heart, and I cannot leave without expressing my warmest thanks. What you said had a special meaning for me not only because you stand for all that is finest in womanhood, but also because your friendship has blessed my life this many a year. It was wonderful to have you speak of the love of the peoples that would welcome me and of my affection for them." HK to Eleanor Roosevelt, February 2, 1955, General Correspondence, 1953–56, Helen Keller file, Eleanor Roosevelt Papers, FERL.

43. *New York Times*, February 4, 1955; Meyerowitz, "Beyond the Feminine Mystique," 1463.

44. Eric Boulter, Field Director, AFOB to Mr. John Stegmaier, Public Affairs Officer, Bureau of Far Eastern Affairs, December 18, 1954, General Records of the Department of State, 1950–1954, Central Decimal File. 032 HK; Foreign Service Dispatch from U.S. Embassy Rangoon, June 3, 1955, General Records of the Department of State, 1950–1954, Central Decimal File. 032 HK.

45. HK to NBH, April 23, 1955, Henney folder, AFB.

46. NBH to HK, HC, PSB. For further information on USIA efforts, see White, *The American Century*, 236–244.

47. HK to NBH, June 8, 1957, Henney folder, AFB. For State Department information on the trip, see: General Records of the Department of State, 1955–1959 Central Decimal File. 511.583/1–357.

48. For example, see HJ, February 21, 1956, April 29, 1960, September 15, 1960, October 7, 1960, October 29, 1960, August 23, 1961, HC, PSB.

49. Lash, *Helen and Teacher*, 762-764, 769–770; Herrmann, *Helen Keller*, 324–326.

50. Lash, *Helen and Teacher*, 769.

NOTES TO CHAPTER 5

1. In 2001, scholar Jodi Cressman counted over 200 published Keller biographies—most of them written for children. Cressman, "Helen Keller and the Mind's Eyewitness."

2. Murphy, *Your Deafness Is Not You.* NBH to PT, August 13, 1954, August 18, 1954, AFB. For other examples, see HJ, February 23, 1956 HC, PSB; NBH to Robert Barnett, March 3, 1957 HC, PSB. For the Lawrence strike reference, see NBH to PT, August 15, 1954, AFB. The book is Cahn, *Mill Town.*

3. HJ, September 24, 1957, HC, PSB. The Tibble book referred to was directed toward elementary school students: J. W. & A. Tibble, *Helen Keller* (New York: G. P. Putnam's Sons, 1954); Hickok's *The Touch of Magic*; the Esther Costello picture was a 1957 film version of *The Story of Esther Costello.* For more on the Costello book (1952), see Lash, *Helen and Teacher,* 732–738.

4. NBH to Ken McCormick, April 24 and 26, 1956, HC, PSB. McCormick went on, saying that "enough has been done on Helen's life recently so that there would have to be a lapse of time before such a book could be published." Ken McCormick to NBH, October 18, 1957, HJ, HC, PSB. Several months later Henney admitted "that I got too panicky about this rash of mediocre books about Helen. I don't suppose they'll do any harm and I think it would be a mistake to rush into anything because of them." NBH to Ken McCormick, February 24, 1958, HJ, HC, PSB.

5. NBH to Ken McCormick, May 10, 1957, HC, PSB. Henney attempted to control who could write on Keller, even after both she and Keller had died. In 1976 and 1977, the AFB sought a writer for what was to result in Joseph Lash's 1980 biography of Keller and included Henney's husband Keith in the discussion. Keith Henney to Marguerite Levine, July 12, 1976, Henney 1975 folder, AFB; Marguerite Levine to Keith Henney, November 15, 1977, Henney 1975 folder, AFB.

6. Robert Barnett to NBH, August 25, 1971, Henney folder, AFB; NBH to Robert Barnett, December 25, 1971, Henney folder, AFB. The book referred to is Harrity and Martin, *The Three Lives of Helen Keller.*

7. Joseph Lash to Mary Ellen Mulholland, Director of Publications, April 29, 1985, Lash folder, AFB. Lash did the book at the request of Radcliffe College and Merloyd Lawrence, the publisher. Marguerite Levine to Keith Henney, November 15, 1977, Henney 1975 folder, AFB. See also Keith Henney to Mrs. Levine, July 12, 1976, Henney 1975 folder, AFB.

8. Barrick, "The Helen Keller Joke Cycle." People with disabilities now create their own disability humor. Like other social groupings (e.g., African Americans, gays and lesbians), people with disabilities are claiming, manipulating, and redefining the

stereotypes about them. These create dialogue about disability by forcing those hearing or reading the humor to acknowledge their own assumptions and attitudes. They also create community, emphasize a shared experience that is devalued by the larger culture, and reject the notion of disability as tragedy. In addition, they also shed light on the random nature of *normality* and the assumptions of able-bodiedness. Contemporary cartoonist, John Callahan, for example, does this in a cartoon in which a two-legged alien is considered disabled by a three-legged alien society. Albrecht, "Disability Humor: What's in a Joke?"

9. Loewen, *Lies My Teacher Told Me*, 26; Klages, "What to Do with Helen Keller Jokes," 18.

10. Klages, "What to Do with Helen Keller Jokes," 20.

11. Barrick, "The Helen Keller Joke Cycle"; Schultz and Germeroth, "Should We Laugh or Should We Cry?"

12. "Give Helen Keller Respect She Deserves," *Toronto Star Newspapers*, June 21, 1998.

13. Klages, "What to Do with Helen Keller Jokes," 18, 22.

14. Ibid., 21–22.

15. HJ, November 29, 1952, HC, PSB. Joseph Lash's interview with Robert Barnett, March 11, 1978; Joseph Lash's interview with Ken McCormick, November 8, 1977; Joseph Lash's interview with Frances Koestler, October 31, 1978; Joseph Lash's interview with Eric Boulter, November 9, 1978; Joseph Lash Papers, box 53, folder 7, FERL.

16. *New York Times*, June 25, 1950.

17. Garland-Thomson, *Extraordinary Bodies*, 29; See also Garland-Thomson, "Feminist Theory, the Body, and the Disabled Figure," 285.

18. Lash, *Helen and Teacher*, 50.

19. Ibid., 216.

20. Laura Bridgman made no effort to do this. Gitter writes that "unlike Keller, Laura never aspired to 'normality' or fostered reassuring illusions. She fully reported her loneliness, frustration, and anger. Unless something pleased or amused her, she saw no reason to smile. Passing for able-bodied never occurred to her: even in an institution for the blind, she had always been the one who was different." Gitter, *The Imprisoned Guest*, 292.

21. Herrmann, *Helen Keller*, 181, 233. For a history of glass eyes, see Ott, "Hard Wear and Soft Tissue."

22. Keller, *Midstream*, 244; Garland-Thomson, "Seeing the Disabled," 347.

23. Keller, *Teacher*, 50.

24. Klages, *Woeful Afflictions*, 193; Davis, *Enforcing Normalcy*, 2.

25. Davis, *Enforcing Normalcy*, 94.

26. Gibson came to Henney once the script was complete and he had already contracted with ABC for a production. He based the play on Anne Sullivan's letters available publicly and widely reprinted. Lash, *Helen and Teacher*, 753–754, 760–765. HJ, August 18, 1959, HC, PSB. The Disney production stars Hallie Kate Eisenberg ("the Pepsi Girl") and is directed by Nadia Tass.

27. Swan, "Touching-Words," 93; Georgina Kleege, "The World in Your Hand: An Open Letter to Helen Keller," unpublished work in process; Klages, *Woeful Afflictions*, 199. See Klages, chapter 9, for a strong and more complete analysis of *The Miracle Worker*.

28. For a description of Georgina Kleege's visit to the Helen Keller home, see Kleege, "The World in Your Hand"; Loewen, *Lies Across America*, 243, 243–245.

29. The plaque outside this crypt shines richly because of all the human hands that pass over the Braille marker.

30. HJ, November/December 1946, HC, PSB.

31. For original plans, see HJ, March 22, 1954, HC, PSB. Regarding the change, see HJ, April 19, 1960, HC, PSB. Whether the break between Henney and Keller was related to this is unclear. Oral history interview with Robert Barnett, March 11, 1978, Joseph Lash Papers, folder 7, FERI. Lash discusses the arrangements for Keller's papers in Lash, *Helen and Teacher*, 753.

32. Associated Press release, October 8, 2001.

33. Loewen, *Lies My Teacher Told Me*, 25.

Bibliography

Albrecht, Gary L. "Disability Humor: What's in a Joke?" *Body & Society* 5/4 (1999): 67–74.

Alonso, Harriet Hyman. *Peace as a Women's Issue: A History of the U.S. Movement for World Peace and Women's Rights*. Syracuse: Syracuse University Press, 1993.

Barrick, Mac E. "The Helen Keller Joke Cycle." *Journal of American Folklore* 93/370 (1980): 441–449.

Baynton, Douglas C. "Disability and the Justification of Inequality in American History." In Paul K. Longmore and Lauri Umansky, eds., *The New Disability History: American Perspectives*. New York: New York University Press, 2001: 33–57.

———. *Forbidden Signs: American Culture and the Campaign against Sign Language*. Chicago: University of Chicago Press, 1996.

———. "The Inspection Line: Disabled Immigrants at the American Border, 1882–1924." Paper delivered at the Organization of American Historians meeting, 1999.

Bell, Daniel. *Marxian Socialism in the United States*. Princeton: Princeton University Press, 1967.

Berghahn, Volker R. "Philanthropy and Diplomacy in the 'American Century.'" *Diplomatic History* 23/3 (Summer 1999): 393–419.

Blaxall, Arthur William. *Helen Keller under the Southern Cross*. Cape Town: Juta, 1952.

Bodgan, Robert. *Freak Show: Presenting Human Oddities for Amusement and Profit*. Chicago: University of Chicago Press, 1988.

Brooks, Van Wyck. *Helen Keller: Sketch for a Portrait*. New York: E. P. Dutton, 1956.

———. *An Autobiography*. New York: E. P. Dutton & Company, 1965.

Buchanan, Robert M. *Illusions of Equality: Deaf Americans in School and Factory, 1850–1950*. Washington: Gallaudet University Press, 1999.

Burch, Susan. *Signs of Resistance: American Deaf Cultural History, 1900 to WWII*. New York: New York University Press, 2002.

Cahn, William. *Mill Town: A Dramatic, Pictorial Narrative of the Century-Old Fight to Unionize an Industrial Town*. New York: Cameron & Kahn, 1954.

Clark, Brett, and John Bellamy Foster. "Helen Keller and the Touch of Nature." *Organization and Environment* 15/3 (September 2002): 278–284.

Classen, Constance. *The Color of Angels: Cosmology, Gender and the Aesthetic Imagination*. New York: Routledge, 1998.

Cohen, Paula Marantz. "Helen Keller and the American Myth." *Yale Review* 85/1 (January 1997): 1–20.

Cotton, Carol. "Helen Keller's First Public Speech." *Alabama Historical Quarterly* 37 (1975): 68–72.

Cressman, Jodi. "Helen Keller and the Mind's Eyewitness." *Western Humanities Review* 54/2 (Fall 2000): 108–123.

Crow, Liz. "Helen Keller: Rethinking the Problematic Icon." *Disability and Society* 15/6 (2000): 845–859.

Crutchfield, Susan. "The Most Wonderful Woman in the World: Language, Assimilation, and American Identity in Helen Keller's 1919 Semi-biographical Film, *Deliverance*." Unpublished paper cited with author's permission.

Davis, Lennard J. *Bending over Backwards: Disability, Dismodernism and Other Difficult Positions*. New York: New York University Press, 2002.

———. *Enforcing Normalcy: Disability, Deafness, and the Body*. New York: Verso, 1995.

Davidson, Jo. *Between Sittings: An Informal Autobiography of Jo Davidson*. New York: Dial Press, 1951.

De Felice, Robert J. "The Crippled Body Speaks." Ph.D. dissertation, State University of New York-Buffalo, 1989.

Diliberto, Gioia. *A Useful Woman: The Early Life of Jane Addams*. New York: Scribner, 1999.

Dower, John. *Embracing Defeat: Japan in the Wake of World War II*. New York: W. W. Norton, 1999.

Early, Frances H. "Feminism, Peace, and Civil Liberties: Women's Role in the Origins of the World War I Civil Liberties Movement." *Women's Studies* 18 (1990): 99–115.

Einhorn, Lois J. *Helen Keller, Public Speaker: Sightless but Seen, Deaf but Heard*. Westport, Conn: Greenwood Press, 1998.

Finger, Anne. "Helen and Frida." In Lennard Davis, ed., *The Disability Studies Reader*. New York: Routledge, 1997: 401–407.

Fishbein, Leslie. *Rebels in Bohemia: The Radicals of the Masses, 1911–1917*. Chapel Hill: University of North Carolina Press, 1982.

Foner, Philip S., ed. *Helen Keller: Her Socialist Years*. New York: International Publishers, 1967.

Freeberg, Ernest. *The Education of Laura Bridgman: First Deaf and Blind Person to Learn Language*. Cambridge: Harvard University Press, 2001.

Gallagher, Hugh Gregory. *FDR's Splendid Deception*. New York: Dodd, Mead, 1985.

Giffin, Frederick C. "The Radical Vision of Helen Keller." *International Social Science Review* 59/4 (1984): 27–32.

Gitter, Elisabeth. *The Imprisoned Guest: Samuel Howe and Laura Bridgman, the Original Deaf-Blind Girl*. New York: Farrar, Straus and Giroux, 2001.

———. "The Blind Daughter in Charles Dickens's *Cricket on the Hearth*." *Studies in English Literature, 1500–1900* 39/4 (1999): 675–689.

Goldman, Emma. *Living My Life*. New York: AMS Press, 1970.

Goode, David. *A World without Words: The Social Construction of Children Born Deaf and Blind*. Philadelphia: Temple University Press, 1994.

Grew, Joseph C. *Ten Years in Japan*. New York: Arno Press, 1972.

Harrity, Richard, and Ralph G. Martin. *The Three Lives of Helen Keller*. Garden City, N.Y.: Doubleday, 1962.

Hay, Stephen N. "Rabindranath Tagore in America." *American Quarterly* 14/3 (Autumn 1962): 439–463.

Heilbrun, Carolyn G. *Writing a Woman's Life*. New York: Ballantine Books, 1989.

Henney, Nella Braddy. *With Helen Keller*. North Conway: North Conway Publishing, 1974.

———. *Anne Sullivan Macy: The Story Behind Helen Keller*. New York: Doubleday, 1933.

Herrmann, Dorothy. *Helen Keller: A Life*. New York: Alfred A. Knopf, 1998.

Hickock, Lorena. *The Touch of Magic: The Story of Helen Keller's Great Teacher, Anne Sullivan Macy*. New York: Dodd, Mead, 1961.

Hillyer, Barbara. *Feminism and Disability*. Norman: University of Oklahoma Press, 1993.

Hutchinson, George B. "Whitman and the Black Poet: Kelly Miller's Speech to the Walt Whitman Fellowship." *American Literature* 61/1 (March 1989): 46–58.

Keller, Helen. *Light in My Darkness*. Revised and edited by Ray Silverman. West Chester, Pa.: Chrysalia Press, 2000 [Revised version of *My Religion*, 1927].

———. *Teacher*. New York: Doubleday, 1955.

———. *Helen Keller's Journal*. London: Michael Joseph, 1938.

———. *Midstream: My Later Life*. New York: Greenwood Press, [1929] 1968.

———. *My Religion*. New York: Citadel Press, [1927], [1960], 1963.

———. *Out of the Dark: Essays, Letters, and Addresses on Physical and Social Vision*. New York: Doubleday, Page, 1914.

———. *The World I Live In*. New York: Century Company, 1908.

———. *The Story of My Life*, New York: Dover Publications, [1903] 1996.

Kerber, Linda K. *No Constitutional Right to Be Ladies: Women and the Obligations of Citizenship*. New York: Hill and Wang, 1998.

Klages, Mary. *Woeful Afflictions: Disability and Sentimentality in Victorian America.* Philadelphia: University of Pennsylvania Press, 1999.

———. "What to Do with Helen Keller Jokes: A Feminist Act." In Regina Barreca, ed., *New Perspectives on Women and Comedy.* Philadelphia: Gordon and Breach, 1992: 13–22.

Kleege, Georgina. "Helen Keller and 'The Empire of the Normal.'" *American Quarterly* 52/2 (June 2000): 322–325.

———. "Blindness and Insight." Raritan 22/2 (Fall 2002): 162–179.

———. "Letters to Helen." *Michigan Quarterly Review.* 37/3 (Summer 1998): 371–391.

———. "Blind Rage." *Southwest Review.* 83/1 (1998): 53–61.

———. "The World in Your Hands: An Open Letter to Helen Keller." Unpublished work in process, cited with author's permission.

———. "Helen Keller's Love Life." Unpublished work in process, cited with author's permission.

Kline, Wendy. *Building a Better Race: Gender, Sexuality, and Eugenics from the Turn of the Century to the Baby Boom.* Berkeley: University of California Press, 2001.

Koestler, Frances A. *The Unseen Minority: A Social History of Blindness in America.* New York: David McKay, 1976.

Kraft, Barbara S. *The Peace Ship: Henry Ford's Pacifist Adventure in the First World War.* New York: Macmillan, 1978.

Kudlick, Catherine J. "The Outlook of *The Problem* and the Problem with the *Outlook*: Two Advocacy Journals Reinvent Blind People in Turn-of-the-Century America." In Paul K. Longmore and Lauri Umansky, eds., *The New Disability History: American Perspectives.* New York: New York University Press, 2001: 187–213.

———. "Helen Keller, American Pragmatism, and French Ideas of Acculturation." Paper presented at the Western Society for French History, 2002. In author's possession.

Ladd-Taylor, Molly. "Eugenics, Sterilization and Modern Marriage in the USA: The Strange Career of Paul Popenoe." *Gender & History* 13/2 (August 2001): 298–327.

Lane, Harlan. *When the Mind Hears: A History of the Deaf.* New York: Vintage Books, 1989.

———. *The Mask of Benevolence: Disabling the Deaf Community.* San Diego: Dawn Sign Press, [1992], 1999.

Lasch, Christopher. *The Social Thought of Jane Addams.* New York: Bobbs-Merrill, 1965.

Lash, Joseph. *Helen and Teacher: The Story of Helen Keller and Anne Sullivan Macy.* New York: Addison-Wesley, 1980.

Lewis, David Levering. *W. E. B. Du Bois: The Fight for Equality and the American Century, 1919–1963*. New York: Henry Holt, 2000.

Linton, Simi. *Claiming Disability: Knowledge and Identity*. New York: New York University Press, 1998.

Loewen, James W. *Lies Across America: What Our Historic Sites Get Wrong*. New York: New Press, 1999.

———. *Lies My Teacher Told Me: Everything Your American History Textbook Got Wrong*. New York: New York University Press, 1995.

Longmore, Paul K., and David Goldberger. "The League of the Physically Handicapped and the Great Depression: A Case Study in the New Disability History." *Journal of American History* 87/3 (December 2000): 888–922.

Longmore, Paul K., and Lauri Umansky. "Disability History: From the Margins to the Mainstream." In Paul K. Longmore and Lauri Umansky, eds., *The New Disability History: American Perspectives*. New York: New York University Press, 2001: 1–29.

———. "A Note on Language and the Social Identity of Disabled People." *American Behavioral Scientist* 18/2 (January/February 1985): 419–423.

———. "The Life of Randolph Bourne and the Need for a History of Disabled People." *Reviews in American History* (December 1985): 581–587.

Macy, John. *About Women*. New York: William Morrow, 1930.

———. *Socialism in America*. New York: Doubleday, 1916.

Meyerowitz, Joanne. "Beyond the Feminine Mystique: A Reassessment of Postwar Mass Culture, 1946–1958." *Journal of American History* 79/4 (March 1993): 1455–1482.

Muncy, Robyn. *Creating a Female Dominion in American Reform, 1890–1935*. New York: Oxford University Press, 1991.

Murphy, Grace. *Your Deafness Is Not You: New Design for Deafness*. New York: Harper, 1954.

Nagai, Takashi. *The Bells of Nagasaki*. New York: Kodansha International, 1984 edition.

Neff, Nelson. "Travels with Helen and Polly." Unpublished manuscript in Nelson Neff file, AFB, 1972.

Nielsen, Kim. *Un-American Womanhood: AntiRadicalism, AntiFeminism, and the First Red Scare*. Columbus: Ohio State University Press, 2001.

———. "Helen Keller and the Politics of Civic Fitness." In Paul Longmore and Lauri Umansky, eds., *The New Disability History: American Perspectives*. New York: New York University Press, 2001: 268–290.

Oldfield, Sybil. *Women Against the Iron Fist: Alternatives to Militarism, 1900–1989*. Oxford, Eng.: Basil Blackwell, 1989.

Ott, Katherine. "Hard Wear and Soft Tissue: Craft and Commerce in Artificial Eyes." In Katherine Ott, David Serlin, and Stephen Mihm, eds., *Artificial Parts, Practical Lives: Modern Histories of Prosthetics*. New York: New York University Press, 2002: 147–170.

Pelka, Fred. "Helen Keller and the FBI." *Ragged Edge* 5 (2001): 19–22, 35, 36.

Pernick, Martin S. *The Black Stork: Eugenics and the Death of "Defective" Babies in American Medicine and Motion Pictures since 1915*. New York: Oxford University Press, 1996.

Porter, Edna, ed. *Double Blossoms: Helen Keller Anthology*. New York: Lewis Copeland, 1931.

Rodgers, Daniel T. *The Work Ethic in Industrial America, 1850–1920*. Chicago: University of Chicago Press, 1974.

Rubin, Barry. *Secrets of State: The State Department and the Struggle over U.S. Foreign Policy*. New York: Oxford University Press, 1987.

Ryan, James Emmett. "The Blind Authoress of New York: Helen De Kroyft and the Uses of Disability in Antebellum America." *American Quarterly* 51/2 (1999): 385–418.

Schor, Naomi. "Blindness as Metaphor." *Différences* 11/2 (1999): 76–105.

Schott, Linda. *Reconstructing Women's Thoughts: The Women's International League for Peace and Freedom before World War II*. Stanford: Stanford University Press, 1997.

Schultz, Kara, and Darla Germeroth. "Should We Laugh or Should We Cry? John Callahan's Humor as a Tool to Change Societal Attitudes Toward Disability." *Howard Journal of Communications* 9 (1998): 229–244.

Selden, Steven. "Eugenics and the Social Construction of Merit, Race, and Disability." *Journal of Curriculum Studies* 32/2 (2000): 235–252.

Shapiro, Joseph P. *No Pity: People with Disabilities Forging a New Civil Rights Movement*. New York: Random House, 1993.

Shklar, Judith N. *American Citizenship: The Quest for Inclusion*. Cambridge, Mass: Harvard University Press, 1991.

Smith, J. David. "The Challenge of Advocacy: The Different Voices of Helen Keller and Burton Blatt." *Mental Retardation* 35/2 (April 1997): 138–140.

Snyder, Robert E. "Women, Wobblies, and Workers' Rights: The 1912 Textile Strike in Little Falls, New York." In Joseph Conlin, ed., *At the Point of Production: The Local History of the IWW*. Westport, Conn: Greenwood Press, 1981, 27–48.

———. "Women, Wobblies, and Workers' Rights: The 1912 Textile Strike in Little Falls, New York." *New York History* 60 (January 1979): 29–57.

Snyder, Sharon L., and David T. Mitchell. "Out of the Ashes of Eugenics: Diagnostic Regimes in the United States and the Making of a Disability Minority." *Patterns of Prejudice* 36/1 (2002): 79–103.

Swan, Jim. "Touching Words: Helen Keller, Plagiarism, Authorship." In Martha Woodmansee and Peter Jaszi, eds., *The Construction of Authorship: Textual Appropriation in Law and Literature*. Durham: Duke University Press, 1994: 57–100.

Symes, Lillian, and Travers Clement. *Rebel America: The Story of Social Revolt in the United States*. New York: Harper & Brothers, 1934.

Thomson, Rosemarie Garland. "The FDR Memorial: Who Speaks from the Wheelchair?" *Chronicle of Higher Education*, January 26, 2001: B11–B12.

———. "Seeing the Disabled: Visual Representations of Disability in Popular Photography." In Paul K. Longmore and Lauri Umansky, eds., *The New Disability History: American Perspectives*. New York: New York University Press, 2001: 335–374.

———. *Extraordinary Bodies: Figuring Physical Disability in American Culture and Literature*. New York: Columbia University Press, 1997.

———. "Feminist Theory, the Body, and the Disabled Figure." In Lennard J. Davis, ed., *The Disability Studies Reader*. New York: Routledge, 1997: 279–292.

Tomlins, Christopher. "Subordination, Authority, Law: Subjects in Labor History." *International Labor and Working-Class History* 47 (Spring 1995): 56–90.

Unger, Nancy. *Fighting Bob La Follette: The Righteous Reformer*. Chapel Hill: University of North Carolina Press, 2000.

Wait, Gary E. "Julia Brace." *Dartmouth College Library Bulletin* 33/1 (November 1992): 2–10.

Waterhouse, Edward J. "Education of the Deaf-Blind in the United States of America, 1837–1967." In Edgar Lowell and Carole Rouin, eds., *State of the Art: Perspectives on Serving Deaf-Blind Children*. Washington, D. C.: U.S. Department of Education, 1977: 5–17.

Wells, H. G. *New Worlds for Old*. New York: MacMillan, 1913.

White, Donald W. *The American Century: The Rise and Decline of the United States as a World Power*. New Haven: Yale University Press, 1996.

Wolfe, Kathi. "Helen Keller." *Mainstream* 20/10 (August 1996): 33–39.

———. "Helen Keller, Radical." *Utne Reader* (July-August 1996): 16.

———. "War Work." *Mainstream* 19/10 (August 1995): 17–23.

Young, Iola. "Helen Keller Came." *Pacific Historian* 24 (1980): 55–59.

Zeiger, Susan. "She Didn't Raise Her Boy to Be a Slacker: Motherhood, Conscription, and the Culture of the First World War." *Feminist Studies* 22/1 (Spring 1996): 7–39.

———. "Finding a Cure for War: Women's Politics and the Peace Movement in the 1920s." *Journal of Social History* 24 (Fall 1990): 69–86.

Index

Addams, Jane, 19, 36, 37, 69
American Civil Liberties Union, 24
American Foundation for the Blind, 8, 13, 46, 78; creation of, 47; employment of Keller, 47–48, 50, 68, 81; fundraising, 7, 48, 50, 51, 85; and Keller's international travel, 100, 111, 115, 119–120; and Keller's politics, 48, 77, 85, 102, 112, 113; lobbying, 7, 22, 50, 52–53; Nobel Peace Prize campaign, 116, 126; shaping of Keller's memory, 113–114, 115–116, 126–128, 140–141
American Foundation for the Overseas Blind, 82, 106, 107
American Rescue Ship Mission, 71–72
American School for the Deaf, 3
American Sign Language, 2, 11
Anagnos, Michael, 1, 3, 6, 7, 8, 10, 20
Anticommunism, 84, 85, 101, 112–113, 115
Arab Jerusalem, 109–110
Australia, 85, 87

Barnett, Robert, 51, 53, 102, 127, 140
Bell, Alexander Graham: deafness, 2; and Keller, 1–3, 7, 8, 10, 13, 22, 41
Birth control, 7, 35
Bollinger baby, 36, 68
Bond, Amelia, 59
Boulter, Eric, 116
Brace, Julia, 3
Braille: Keller's use of, 43, 64; Nazi restriction of, 71
Braille, Louis, 112
Brazil, 114, 115
Bridgman, Laura, 3, 6, 7, 8, 20
Brooks, Van Wyck, 8, 76
Bunche, Ralph, 103
Burma, 96, 118, 119–120

Canada, 120
Carlson, Lane, 88
Carnegie, Andrew, 32–33
Chile, 73, 114
China, 67, 86, 96, 118
Colan, Elaine, 68–69
Corbally, Winifred, 123

Cornell, Katharine, 75, 83, 85, 113, 121
Crum, Bartley, 106

Davidson, Jo, 79, 82, 83, 84, 103, 104; death, 106; friendship with Keller, 73–75, 76, 100–101; politics, 77, 106; Wallace campaign, 84–85, 86
Debs, Eugene V., 24, 27
Deliverance (film), 41–42
Denmark, 120
Dickens, Charles, 3
Disability: cultural attitudes about, 9–10, 15, 16, 41, 49–50, 68–69, 78–79, 87, 118–119, 141; and employment, 11, 28–32, 69, 78–79, 89; and industrialization, 7, 23–24; politics of, 9–10. *See also* Helen Keller jokes; Keller, Helen, disability; Keller, Helen, questions regarding her capabilities
Disability studies, 13
Disabled veterans, 11, 77–79, 82

Egypt, 85, 96, 100, 106, 107, 108
England, 82
Eugenics, 36–37, 49, 69; Keller's opinions on, 11, 36–37, 40, 41

Fagan, Peter, 40–41, 55
Female suffrage, 7, 10, 35
Finger-spelling, 2, 3, 116, 135
Finland, 120
Finley, John, 66, 67, 70–71
Ford, Henry, 37–38
Foundation for the Overseas Blind. *See* American Foundation for the Overseas Blind
France, 82, 100, 112

Gibson, William, 136. See also *Miracle Worker, The*
Giovannitti, Arturo, 18, 25, 27, 48
Goldman, Emma, 46
Greece, 82
Grummons, Stuart and Sandra, 75, 76
Gurion, David Ben, 110

Haas, Herbert, 63, 101–102
Haiselden, Harry, Dr., 36–37, 68

175

About the Author

Historian KIM E. NIELSEN is Associate Professor of Social Change and Development at the University of Wisconsin-Green Bay, where she teaches courses in History and Women's Studies. She is also the author of *Un-American Womanhood: Antiradicalism, Antifeminism, and the First Red Scare.*